The Presence of the Past
in Modern American Drama

FAIRLEIGH DICKINSON UNIVERSITY PRESS AWARDS

Beyond the Ballot Box: A Social History of the Boston Irish, 1845–1917
  By Dennis P. Ryan

The Hieroglyphic King: Wisdom and Idolatry in the Seventeenth-Century Masque
  By Stephen Kogan

Images of Victorian Womanhood in English Art
  By Susan P. Casteras

The Presence of the Past in Modern American Drama
  By Patricia R. Schroeder

The Presence of the Past in Modern American Drama

Patricia R. Schroeder

Rutherford ● Madison ● Teaneck
Fairleigh Dickinson University Press
London and Toronto: Associated University Presses

Associated University Presses
440 Forsgate Drive
Cranbury, NJ 08512

Associated University Presses
25 Sicilian Avenue
London WC1A 2QH, England

Associated University Presses
P.O. Box 488, Port Credit
Mississauga, Ontario
Canada L5G 4M2

The paper used in this publication meets the requirements of the American National Standard for Permanence of Paper for Printed Library Materials Z39.48-1984.

Library of Congress Cataloging-in-Publication Data

Schroeder, Patricia Richard.

The presence of the past in modern American drama.

Bibliography: p.
Includes index.
1. American drama—20th century—History and criticism.   2. Memory in literature.   3. History in literature.   I. Title.
PS338.M44S37   1989   812'.5'09353   87-46427
ISBN 0-8386-3332-3 (alk. paper)

Printed in the United States of America

Contents

Acknowledgments

Thornton Wilder once commented that theatre is a collaborative art form, depending for its magic on the combined forces of playwright, director, actors, and audience. This book on theatre is not exactly collaborative, since I maintain full responsibility for its contents, including any errors in fact or judgment and any infelicities of style. Nonetheless, the book would never have been completed without the assistance and expertise of a large number of others, to whom I owe a debt of gratitude.

Foremost among them is Austin E. Quigley, who has had an inestimable effect on the way I think about drama. During the initial stages of this project his penetrating criticism enabled me repeatedly to refine ideas, while his enthusiastic encouragement convinced me that such further refinements were worth the effort. His unshakable confidence in me and in this project cannot be repaid. He has my deepest respect and heartfelt thanks.

A number of others helped me through the arduous thinking and writing processes that led to this book. In particular, I thank David M. Wyatt, an immensely articulate scholar who never tires of discussing ideas; Raymond V. Nelson, who suffers neither fools nor stylistic barbarisms lightly; and Arnold Aronson, whose thorough knowledge of theatre history saved me from some oversimplifications of fact in an early draft of this work. Several of my colleagues at Ursinus College helped me by responding to various drafts of chapters; for this favor I thank John L. Cobbs, Joyce Henry, and especially Mary K. Tiryak.

For technical help in producing the manuscript I am grateful to Bonnie Price for typing and to Peter Jessup, whose mastery of computer technology and whose generosity with his time shortened my working hours considerably. I am also indebted to the reference staff at Myrin Library of Ursinus College and to Lisa Tremper Barnes, Nancy Francis, and Frank B. Everett.

The editorial and production staffs of Fairleigh Dickinson University Press and Associated University Presses have also been extremely helpful. I am grateful to Harry Keyishian for encouragement, Lauren Lepow for superb editing, June Schlueter for thoughtful suggestions, and Julien Yoseloff and Beth Gianfagna for patience in answering my numerous questions.

It is a pleasure to acknowledge Ursinus College for generous support of this project.

An early version of my fourth chapter appeared in slightly different form as "Arthur Miller: Illuminating Process" in *REAL* 3 (1985): 265–93. I gratefully acknowledge the publisher's permission to reprint this material.

Finally, I owe gratitude and much more to my husband, Richard G. Schroeder, whose love and support make all things possible. Despite everything, and to my perpetual amazement, he always thinks well of me.

The Presence of the Past
in Modern American Drama

1

An Endless Retrograde Movement

The Perpetual Present

The drama has a unique relationship to time. Stage action necessarily takes place in the present; it unfolds minute by minute, as the audience watches, and thereby embodies time in a way unavailable to nondramatic art forms. This immediacy, of course, is one component of the theatre's enduring greatness; as Thornton Wilder has observed, the glory of the stage is that it is always "now" there.[1] But the eternal present of stage time can also hinder playwrights from exploring complex relationships between the past and the present. As Peter Szondi has described the problem, dramatic action "always occurs in the present. . . . [T]he present passes effecting a change, and from its antitheses there arises a new and different present. The passage of time in the drama is an absolute succession of 'presents'."[2]

Given this "absolute succession of presents," it seems obvious that portraying the past on the stage becomes a crucial problem for a playwright. The problem, however, has rarely been studied in depth, and critical neglect of this issue seems peculiar. After all, the novelist's related problem of depicting the passage of time has been thoroughly investigated; flashbacks, stream-of-consciousness narration, and achronology are now commonplace in fiction and widely recognized as fruitful points of inquiry into the world of a novel. In poetry, too, shifts in time and viewpoint have become standard practice. Yet the past's relationship to the present in the drama, where the demands of performance and the limitations of stage time actually accentuate the issue, has been largely ignored. Even Keir Elam's recent provocative study of theatrical semiotics, which isolates four "temporal levels" in the drama, does so "excluding actual performance time" and so neglects a unique and significant component of the drama's temporal dimension.[3] It also omits any real exploration of the practical methods dramatists have used to depict time on the stage—however many "levels" it entails.

One possible reason that this topic has been largely overlooked is the exceptional conventionality of the theatre. For many playwrights and drama theorists, connecting past to present has seemed merely a matter of exposition—that is, of finding the simplest technique for bringing the audience up to date so that the action can commence. A careful investigation of how past is related to present dramatically, however, will show that simple exposition of past facts is a very small part of the problem. Lurking beneath the apparently simple technical difficulty of how to explain preceding events to the audience is a host of related aesthetic and philosophical conundrums.

First the playwright must decide what the past actually entails. Is the past a series of objective facts and prior events? Sometimes the answer is a simple yes, in which case "exposition" suffices. Other times, however, the past is not entirely a sequence of facts but a matter of recollection and interpretation. In these cases, do all the characters agree about what happened in the past, or do their memories color their notions of it? If the latter, the playwright faces even more decisions. He or she must determine if any one character's interpretation is more valid than those of the others, if all viewpoints contain elements of both truth and fantasy, and if those seemingly factual prior events are objectifiable at all.

Once the playwright has defined the nature of the past by struggling with these complicated issues, he or she must answer the related question of how that past is connected to the present. Did specific, anterior events precipitate the present action of the play, thereby connecting past to present causally as well as sequentially? If so, are the past causes of present actions apparent to any or all of the characters? If not, what past events are significant, and significant in what ways and to whom? A playwright clearly has a number of important choices to make before even selecting those past incidents that need to be included in the present stage time.

Determining the exact relationship between past and present, however, only uncovers the technical problem of how and when to make the past known to the audience. Do the spectators need to know past facts to understand present action? If so, information about prior events must be presented during the opening scenes. Is the audience to be kept in suspense—to share, perhaps, a character's ignorance of past secrets? If so, revelation of the past must be withheld until a later scene. And finally, what *techniques* can a playwright use to introduce necessary past information into the perpetual present of the play? This question is probably the most difficult to answer, since it presupposes answers to all the preceding questions. The dramatist has a large number of traditional expository devices at hand—from heralds and messengers to a chorus of elders to a narrator—but the exact method chosen will depend on the nature of the past that the playwright has chosen and on the particular relationship between past and present posited by the play.

Devising methods for infusing the present with appropriate knowledge of the past became an especially critical problem for twentieth-century American playwrights, who confronted a conflicting double tradition. On the one hand, they inherited the perennial American burden of a complex, partially unfixable past that not only affects the present but partially constitutes it. On the other hand, they inherited a set of dramatic conventions that inhibited their exploring the past's invasion of the present, conventions that permitted mere "exposition" of a past that was radically separate from the present.

In order to understand the extent of this American playwrights' dilemma and the importance of their various solutions to it, it will be necessary to review briefly the conventional methods for connecting past to present that these playwrights inherited. It will also be necessary to explore the vision of the past typical of American literature and to see why this vision prompted innovation in American dramatic form.

Exposing the Past

In each era of dramatic history, playwrights have developed their own "agreed-upon falsehoods" (Thornton Wilder's term for dramatic conventions) for including the past in the present time of the stage. In each case these methods grew out of the prevailing notion of the past's impact on the present and, in turn, helped determine that prevailing notion for future generations of playwrights.[4]

The classical Greek tragedians—a dramatist's earliest models—were able to sidestep many of the problems faced by later playwrights because they had developed a tradition of dramatic irony. Since Greek audiences already knew both the background to and the outcome of the events being enacted, and since everyone agreed that prior choices had directly caused present tragedy, the playwright needed to introduce only that past information which underscored the inevitability of the present action. Everyone in the theatre knew that Oedipus had murdered his own father; likewise, everyone knew that Oedipus's past action was the cause of the plague besetting Thebes as the play begins. The issue for these playwrights, then, was not deciding what sort of past information was important to the unfolding action or how that information might be connected to the present, but rather devising the structural methods that best demonstrated the causal relationship between past and present. In essence, the audience's familiarity with the stories enabled playwrights to concentrate on devising expository *techniques*. Yet the techniques they constructed are of major importance in dramatic history because they set in place a practical tradition of connecting past to present that constrained as well as empowered future generations of playwrights.

Because the past in classical Greek plays is thus necessary but not open to dispute, Greek dramatists developed a number of devices to serve the simple function of objectively reporting the past. The Chorus, for example, was a nostalgic group, given to reminiscing about recent events or reminding slipshod rulers of the 'gods' laws. A number of heralds, messengers, shepherds, and watchmen also remained on hand to keep the principals informed of implied offstage action—including those prior incidents which generated the present dramatic situation of the play. Sometimes even the gods themselves, with their supreme knowledge of time past and time present, would appear to set the scene.

The classical Roman writers borrowed much of their playcrafting technique (and much else as well) from the ancient Greeks, but the past in the Roman plays differs significantly from the publicly known, inescapable past of the Greeks. For the Roman writers, the past consisted of anterior events that directly initiated present action but which, unlike the past of the Greek tragedians, were unknown to the audience. Since the spectators needed immediate information about the events leading up to the play's action, the Roman plays typically began with a retrospective monologue delivered directly to the audience. That such a simple narration could bring the past forward suggests the concrete, verifiable nature of the past in these plays as well as its linear, causal relationship to the present.

This tradition continued in Italian drama through the eighteenth century. Machiavelli's prologue in *Mandragola* tells a story very similar to that introduced by Plautus's Arcturus in *The Rope*, and he tells it in a similar narrative fashion. The seventeenth-century French playwrights borrowed their concept of the past from the Italian writers and continued to begin plays with expository devices (such as gossiping courtiers) designed simply to bring the audience up to date. In both these continental models, the past of which the Greeks needed only reminding was replaced by a past not previously known to the spectators. In both cases, however, specific, factual events in the past still directly caused the onstage action, so the plays had to begin by explaining those antecedent events to the audience. Exposition of an agreed-upon past became more and more a function of the opening scene; the past was thus increasingly isolated from the present action.

In England the drama developed along somewhat different lines. Although the British drama eventually incorporated many of these continental concepts and techniques (as the dominance of the well-made play in the nineteenth century attests), it also grew out of a native tradition that would complicate the prevailing notion of the past's impact on the present. This tradition eventually had profound repercussions on the drama developed by its American heirs.

The British dramatic tradition emerged from two medieval forms: the Corpus Christi cycle plays (also known as pageant plays or mystery plays) and the morality plays. The Corpus Christi plays celebrated the central event of Christianity—Christ's Resurrection—in two ways: by showing its significance in broad historical terms (that is, by linking it to the Creation, Fall, and Last Judgment stories that reveal its ultimate importance); and by demonstrating that the lives of certain Old Testament figures parallel and prefigure it.[5] The cycle thus depicted two sorts of temporal relationships at once: the historical sequence of God's creation and the coexistence of all events in God's mind.[6] Both the cyclic structure of these plays (with repeated patterns and purposeful anachronisms) and their panoramic staging reflected this medieval collapsing of the distinction between past and present.

The morality plays, too, reflected the prevailing vision of time as both concurrent and sequential: by weaving together two distinct yet parallel plots, the morality plays typically suggested the temporal interconnectedness of all events. They also frequently focused on psychological conflicts, thereby developing the need for conventions that would give outward dramatic expression to idiosyncratic versions of both past and present. As a result of this more flexible vision of time's passage, the causality that dominated the Greek stage and its continental descendants was no longer the primary method of relating past to present.

The conventions of the Elizabethan stage have most of their roots in this medieval British tradition. Panoramic staging, a multipurpose set, the use of double plots, direct addresses to the audience—all these conventions depend on a particular sense of history, a particular sort of relationship between past and present, and all dictate a certain set of expository techniques. The Elizabethan prologues, inductions, dumb shows, asides, soliloquies, and plays-within-plays worked within both the tradition of temporal simultaneity and that of historical progress and so provided Shakespeare and his contemporaries with numerous methods for constructing and exploring alternative connections betwen past and present. And although this tradition of flexibility and exploration was rather short-lived within the overall context of dramatic history, it did establish a set of conventions for depicting nonlinear stage time that playwrights of subsequent generations have occasionally restored. Linear causality was no longer the only option for connecting past to present.

The Tyranny of the Well-Made Play

On the continent, however, this tradition of seeing multiple relationships between past and present never really took hold. In fact, with the advent of formal realism in France in the early nineteenth century, the options for exploring the past's impact on the present were intentionally restricted. The apron stage was foreshortened and enclosed within the proscenium arch; the set was designed to replicate as closely as possible the offstage social world.

Within the newly boxed-in stage, separated from the audience by an imaginary fourth wall, the logic of events reigned supreme: playwrights directed their energies toward creating convoluted plots based on the external conflicts of a publicly shared reality and on following Scribe's rigid formula for depicting them. It was, as Stephen S. Stanton has pointed out, a return to the classical tradition, but modified and codified by Scribe's insistence on probability and causal logic, and lacking in audience familiarity or divine intervention.[7] Every situation in these formally realistic plays is prepared for in advance and grows logically out of what has gone before. The past reported on this proscenium stage was chosen precisely to demonstrate the flawless causal logic of a present action that follows surprisingly but inevitably from preceding events. Here, the temporal problems that would specifically beset twentieth-century American playwrights, who recognized a more complex vision of the past at the same time that they inherited the dramatic conventions of formal realism, grew and multiplied.

This plot-centered drama, with its notion of a past causally related to but distant in time from the subsequent present, was transplanted to the English-speaking world in the late nineteenth century, where T. W. Robertson, Sir Arthur Wing Pinero, and Henry Arthur Jones popularized it, and American playwrights unabashedly copied it. The major structural problem they inherited was how to incorporate realistically into the present a persuasively comprehensive version of the past. Within the framework of stage realism, the devices of exposition were, of course, expected to harmonize with the persistent attempt to portray the actions of everyday reality. The English writers accordingly began to replace the asides and soliloquies of their native tradition with the expository devices of formal realism, such as dialogues in which characters tell each other what both already know, gossiping servants who allow the audience to eavesdrop, and dramatically functionless confidants with whom the principals discuss their problems. The creaking of this mechanical plotting seems less than "realistic" to modern playwrights and audiences, but the theatregoing public of the late nineteenth and early twentieth centuries delighted in its intricacies; with few exceptions, they saw no awkwardness in the opening of such plays as Pinero's *The Second Mrs. Tanqueray,* in which the host of a dinner party excuses himself from the table to write a few letters, allowing his dinner guests (who disappear forever after the first act) to discuss their host's predicament for the audience's benefit. Since Pinero's play became something of a cause célèbre in contemporary discussions of expository techniques, it is worth looking in some detail at the several issues the play raised—issues that became increasingly important for twentieth-century American dramatists who inherited Pinero's stage techniques but not his vision of the past.

Although the playwrights and drama theorists of this era rarely questioned the nature of the past they were attempting to portray, many of them recognized the difficulties of constructing a carefully planned exposition within the conventions of formal realism. George Bernard Shaw, for one, was painfully aware of the contrivances of the well-made play, and, despite the workings of its formulas in many of his own plays, he criticized them harshly in the plays of others. Pinero especially suffered under this censorious scrutiny, as Shaw's famous 1895 review of *The Second Mrs. Tanqueray* demonstrates:

> Stage craft, after all, is very narrowly limited by the physical conditions of stage representation; but when one turns over the pages of The Second Mrs. Tanqueray, and notes the naive machinery of the exposition in the first act, in which two whole actors are wasted on sham parts, and the hero, at his own dinner party, is compelled to get up and go ignominiously into the next room "to write some letters" when something has to be said behind his back; when one follows Cayley Drummle, the confidant to whom both Paula and her husband explain themselves for the benefit of the audience . . . it is impossible to avoid the conclusion that what most of our critics mean by mastery of stage craft is recklessness in the substitution of dead machinery and lay figures for vital action and characters.[8]

Shaw's analysis not only aptly sums up the artificiality of contemporary methods for revealing the past but also anticipates the reforms in dramatic structure that were soon to occur.

Shaw's contemporaries seem not to have agreed with him on *The Second Mrs. Tanqueray*, however, for Pinero's play was frequently held up as a model for aspiring young playwrights, its "naive machinery of exposition" praised in the best-known playwriting handbooks. William Archer, for example, in his 1912 "manual of craftsmanship" entitled *Playmaking*, informs his readers that,

> When an exposition cannot be thoroughly dramatized—that is, wrung out, in the stress of the action, from the characters primarily concerned—it may best be dismissed, rapidly and even conventionally, by any not too improbable device.[9]

Professor George Baker (whose pupils in a Harvard playwrighting class included Eugene O'Neill) also addresses the difficulties of exposition in his 1919 handbook *Dramatic Technique*. Baker defines good expository devices as being clear, natural, interesting, and swift; he scoffs at outdated, "unnatural" devices such as the dumb show, the chorus, and the soliloquy; and he mocks such "early steps on the advance of the Chorus" as garrulous servants, cardboard confidants, and "lately, the telephone, the stenographer, and most recently, the dictaphone."[10]

To help his readers avoid such clumsy exposition, Professor Baker urges them to employ "that art which conceals art, for an audience resents a mere recital of necessary facts."[11] His model of art-concealing art is, however, *The Second Mrs. Tanqueray.* Despite his injunctions against inquisitive strangers and convenient confidants, Baker admires the timely arrival of Cayle Drummle; despite his rule that the facts of the past must emerge naturally, he ignores completely the ungentlemanly way Aubrey neglects his dinner guests when a sudden urge to write letters possesses him. He sees only the difficulties of bringing past facts forward into the present and the success with which Pinero's first act dispenses "much needed information" to "the minds of the audience."[12]

The notion of the past applauded by these critics and portrayed by the playwrights they describe is one composed of external facts that precipitate the present action of the plot: it is a past consisting of indisputable causal sequences and "much needed information," a linear past that their "not too improbable" expository devices were designed to reveal. But the rejection of expository devices that failed to satisfy the demands of formal realism was also, it turned out, a rejection of devices that would enable playwrights to explore relationships between past and present other than those of linear causality.

Within this nineteenth-century stage world, where the present action depended upon the causal logic of anterior events, the beginning of the play became the primary locus for exposition of the past. And since all events, past and present, were connected by cause and effect, deciding at what point in the story to begin the play became increasingly dificult. S. H. Butcher, in his classic 1894 translation of and commentary on Aristotle's *Poetics,* tried to apply Aristotelian principles to the contemporary problem of where and how to begin a play. According to Butcher:

> The beginning of the drama is, no doubt, the natural sequel of something else. Still it must not carry us back in thought to all that has gone before.

Antecedent events do not thrust themselves on us in an unending series. Certain facts are necessarily given. We do not trace each of these facts back to its origin, or follow the chain of cause and effect *ad infinitum*. If we did, the drama would become an endless retrograde movement.[13]

Butcher's comment reflects much of the attitude toward drama current in his time: he stresses the causal logic of the plot, the factual nature of the past, and the necessity of forward-moving action. But despite his typically Victorian understanding of the mechanisms of plot construction, Butcher also draws attention (albeit unwillingly, as his definition of the past as "certain facts" indicates) to an important concern of subsequent playwrights: if the chain of prior causality is potentially endless, the process of *selecting* particular shaping events from a character's past and *demonstrating* their complex consequences becomes crucial in determining the nature of the present.

Once one recognizes that the vision of the past depicted on the stage is necessarily selected and abridged, alternative possibilities for defining that past and its relationship to the present emerge rapidly. What if the past is not something "given" (either by gods or causal necessity), but something individuals have a chance to control? What if the characters themselves determine which bits of past information are important, or interpret what appears to be simple temporal sequence according to their own notions of causality? Or, to take the process a step further: What if past causal events are not even recognized as such, by any or all of the characters? What if the search for those past incidents that have caused the present circumstances are permitted to dominate present action? From this recognition of the choices involved in defining and then exposing the past, it takes only a modest creative leap to imagine a drama in which those carefully chosen past incidents are both more and less than facts, a drama in which the memories of the characters, reliable or not, are permitted to determine the spectators' understanding of what has happened in the past. In such a play, speculation about the past could *become* present action. The movement of such a play could, indeed, become "endlessly retrograde," as the characters seek to justify their present actions by selectively characterizing their own and each other's pasts.

This is exactly what happened in the American drama of the twentieth century: the formally realistic expository devices that worried Butcher and his contemporaries became the center of a new experimental trend in the American version of formal realism. Until this time, American dramatists had cheerfully copied the popular conventions of the European stage. The most popular plays of the turn-of-the-century American theatre—James Herne's domestic dramas, David Belasco's romances, and Clyde Fitch's social comedies— all depended on the unremitting cause-and-effect logic of the French Scribean formula and the melodramatic conventions of the British *Black Ey'd Susan* school. Even when the setting, language, and subject matter seemed decidedly American to contemporary audiences, the playwrights imported their dramatic forms. But for some young American playwrights, the past depicted on the formally realistic stage seemed contrived, mechanical, and at variance with contemporary ideas of the past's lingering hold on the present.

The American Past

It is not surprising that American dramatists' first important structural experiments should attempt to connect past to present in new ways: the nature of the past and its influence on the present have been obsessive concerns of American writers since the Pilgrims arrived. In fact, the attitude of the early Puritan settlers toward history contains the seeds of a confusing dualism that still pervades and perhaps defines American literature.[14] The Puritans came to the New World to *create* a new world; their writings and actions bespoke a conscious desire to break away from conventions and the old social order, to disown the past, to begin again. At the same time, their sense of their importance in establishing a model religious community—"a city on a hill," in Governor John Winthrop's phrase— encouraged them to record every event for posterity, that is, to write a *new* history. As Cleanth Brooks, R. W. B. Lewis, and Robert Penn Warren explain this impulse, for the Puritans "every earthly event, however seemingly casual, was a part of God's timeless and all-encompassing plan; and, as such, it had to be scrupulously reported and carefully interpreted."[15] These early colonists were, therefore, a people eschewing history—escaping the past—while simultaneously writing history anew, from a new viewpoint.[16]

What Lewis has called "the legend of a second chance" thus became one of the defining myths in American culture.[17] The early settlers of all the colonies as well as visitors to them remarked on

Americans' peculiar freedom from a past. As Hector St. John de Crèvecoeur described him in 1782,

> *He* is an American, who, leaving behind him all his ancient prejudices and manners, receives new ones from the new mode of life he has embraced, the new government he obeys, and the new rank he holds. . . . The American is a new man, who acts upon new principles.[18]

In 1839 the *Democratic Review* proclaimed that "our national birth was the beginning of a new history . . . which separates us from the past."[19] Throughout the nineteenth century Emerson, Thoreau, and Whitman wrote frequently about the need to renounce the past and to escape subservience to tradition. In short, this decisive repudiation of the past became a leitmotif in American writing.

The American preoccupation with this ideal of pastlessness is both pervasive and profound, but it should not be overemphasized. To do so would be to miss the complexity of the American attitude toward the past and so underestimate the problems of connecting past to present that twentieth-century American playwrights eventually faced. Just as the Puritans troubled to write histories even as they disavowed the tyranny of the past, so many nineteenth-century Americans feared losing the ties to the past that Emerson and Thoreau gloried in evading.

American writers were preoccupied with the past, certainly, but their attitudes toward its nature and its importance were complex and often contradictory. Writers like Irving and Cooper were busy creating a *literary* past for America.[20] By mythologizing the legends and traditions of recent American events (the founding of the Republic, the settling of the West), these writers were able to replace the missing historical past with a "usable" literary past. Even Emerson, that master proselytizer of reliance on self rather than on tradition, was so vociferous in his outcry only because he saw his era becoming too dependent on the past. As he lamented in "Nature" (1836): "Our age is retrospective. It builds the sepulchres of the fathers. It writes biographies, histories, and criticism. The foregoing generation beheld God face to face; we, through their eyes."[21]

Others, like Hawthorne and Melville, built their careers by exploring the effects of memory, history, and tradition—or, even more importantly, on the often disastrous *lack* of such guidelines—on their characters. The typical nineteenth-century American character is a creature without a past, afloat without a tradition, forced to survive through wits and willpower in a hostile, untamed world. And survive this character did, in the literary forms of Natty Bumppo, Hester Prynne, Ishmael, and, later, Thomas Sutpen: all characters, as Fitzgerald would define Jay Gatsby, created by their own Platonic conceptions of themselves. Lacking a sense of either a meaningful personal history or a place in the nation's annals, these characters created mythic identities for themselves to compensate for their often debilitating alienation from the past.

The coming of the industrial age and the discoveries of modern psychology changed the emphasis in American writers' understanding of the past's relationship to the present, but these changes only enhanced its importance. After the rupture in national and historical identity begun by the Civil War and continued by rapid industrialization, urban growth, and immigration, American writers began to observe and lament the seemingly definitive split between past truths and present uncertainties. Rootlessness and separation from history came less and less to suggest joyous self-reliance, and more and more to reflect isolation and alienation. Twentieth-century heroes, perceiving their era to be without absolute values, sought desperately to reclaim the lost values of the past, or, at least, to come to terms with their personal histories, failures included. Whether this entailed recovering the historical and literary past, as T.S. Eliot did, in fragments shored against the ruins of the present, or destroying the past, as William Carlos Williams did, in order to recreate it anew from a personal blueprint, American artists now recognized the absolute necessity of coming to terms with the past and grounding their own visions in examples from history. Henry Adams, Quentin Compson, and Gerontion became the modern American heroes—all characters with an instinct for belief and nothing but the irrecoverable past to believe in.

In this new era of uncertainty, coming to terms with what has been became the only viable way for American writers and their characters to understand the confusion of what is. Deciding exactly what has been, however, became increasingly problematic. As the nature of the past became more obscure and its relationship to the present more difficult to determine, exploration of the possibilities became a compelling literary theme.

This complex and shifting attitude toward the past is, of course, not uniquely American in the twentieth century. The studies of thinkers like Darwin, Freud, Jung, and Nietzsche have by now undermined forever the simplistic notion of the past as something factual and of history as an indisputable chain of events. As Charles Beard explained it as long ago as 1933:

> Contemporary thought about history . . . repudiates the conception domi-nant among schoolmen during the latter part of the nineteenth century and the opening years of the twentieth century—the conception that it is possible to describe the past as it actually was.[22]

Yet the perennial American ambivalence toward the past—what it is, how it affects us, whether we should embrace it, renounce it, recreate it—does help explain why American playwrights of the early twen-tieth century were sensitive enough to its complexities to make it a major focus for structural innovation, despite their reliance on the conventions of formal realism in virtually every other aspect of play-crafting. Attuned to exploring the past by national preoccupation as well as by new international ideas, they were able to see very clearly that the past is not necessarily something separate from the present.

The Past in the Present: An Emerging American Drama

With the founding of the Provincetown Players and the Theatre Guild in 1915, the American theatre began to break away from the conventional realism of its imported models. For writers like Susan Glaspell, the young Eugene O'Neill, and their contemporaries in the group theatre movement, shopworn conventions for summarizing a sequential, causal, agreed-upon past produced a limited and outdated picture of reality. But how could a playwright, working on a formally realistic stage that exists in the perpetual present, depict a past that not only sets the plot in motion but also partially constitutes and partially controls the present? The past as anterior action had to give way to the past as a functioning component of present stage reality. The age demanded a new dramatic form.

To be sure, these young American dramatists had a few recent models to follow, models whose dramatic methods could help launch their own theatrical experiments. Foremost among them was Henrik Ibsen, whose technique of retrospective analysis would influence American playwrights (most notably O'Neill and Miller) for over half a century. Although Ibsen's plays retained most of the conventional devices of Scribean realism, Ibsen anticipated American dramatists' concern with the past's continuing influence on the present, and he reclaimed a structural method to portray it. Ibsen's method, like that of the ancient Greeks, depends on choosing a starting point for a play close to the climax of the action; from that point, the play's present action progressively explores preceding events, gradually revealing the incidents that precipitated the present crisis before portraying the crisis itself.[23] For young American playwrights who no longer viewed the past as something to be isolated in an opening scene, this retrospective method of intermingling past with present would prove to be quite useful.

Ibsen's dramatic method provided only a partial solution to the problem, however. His retrospective analysis accounted for the past's continuing impact on the present and offered a technique for demonstrating that impact. But the notion of the past crucial to Ibsen's realistic plays is still one of completed, preceding events. Nora's forgery, Werle's criminal business practices, and Osvald's inherited disease compose the past of Ibsen's stage reality, a past in which secret sins and hidden crimes come back to haunt the characters. To construct a different sort of stage past—a past partially interior, partially irrecoverable, significant in sometimes indecipherable ways, and often inseparable from the present—O'Neill and his contemporaries turned to another set of models: August Strindberg and the German expressionists, such as Georg Kaiser and Ernst Toller, whose plays were frequently produced in New York during the early 1900s.

The German expressionist playwrights, disciples of Strindberg, developed a dramatic form that emphasized interior reality and personal vision (either that of a character or that of the artist) rather than objective facts. Using symbolic rather than conventionally realistic settings, episodic rather than cause-and-effect structure, suggestive rather than mimetic action, abstract rather than specific characters, and peripatetic, multifunctioning dialogue rather than drawing-room conversation, they created a stage world designed to contrast with the offstage world replicated so tidily by the realists. In this dream world the dreamer rules, constructing the plot according to internal logic, defining the present primarily by personal emotions and recollections. The dreamer becomes the central subject of the play as well as the object of its inquiries. The need to authenticate the past by conventional means—a cardboard confidant, a gossiping servant—disappears, as the character's conception of the past becomes the past that matters most. The expressionistic stage more closely resembled that of the Elizabethans, with its multiple devices for exploring interior reality, than it did the formally realistic stage.

Critics and historians have long recognized the lingering effects of expressionism on the American drama. One reads that expressionism is a "motivating force" in American drama or a "crystallization of the spirit of the age."[24] In their enthusiasm for this genuinely influential movement, however, many critics have overestimated its actual impact on the American stage. In fact, true expressionism remained in vogue only briefly, and its consequences were limited. Unlike European drama of the twentieth century, which by and large abandoned the structures of formal realism in favor of more wide-ranging, experimental forms, the drama in America has retained its realistic format and has supplemented rather than replaced it with expressionistic devices. Very few important American plays—probably only Elmer Rice's *Adding Machine*, O'Neill's *Emperor Jones*, and Williams's *Camino Real*—can truly be called "expressionistic" in the original sense of the word.

Much of the critical overemphasis occurs because "expressionism" has been used as a generic term for all antimimetic devices. It is, rather, the name of a particular literary form based on a particular philosophy and armed with an arsenal of particular techniques.[25] This seemingly inconsequential misnomer has obscured the particular ways American playwrights have used specific expressionistic techniques. In fact, the characteristically realistic American drama has absorbed from expressionism mainly those devices that manipulate time and causality, thereby realizing one structural solution to their persistent problem of exploring the past. By using expressionistic devices to depict the past concurrently with the present, American playwrights have been able to dramatize expository scenes that would otherwise have been presented through artfully concealed narrations or some other "not too improbable device." And as a result, these scenes from the past are no longer simply expository, but a core part of the ongoing action.

In essence, expressionism was important to modern American drama because it provided a method for revealing interior reality and so postulated alternative visions of the past. It also provided alternative means for portraying that past and devices that permitted the past to permeate the present as well as precede it. And combined with

Ibsen's version of retrospective formal realism, expressionism paved the way for the temporally flexible but otherwise formally realistic stage world constructed by America's most important playwrights, a world capable of supporting a widened range of human experience. Unlike their European counterparts, American playwrights have never really relinquished the conventions of formal realism, but they continue to experiment with devices for presenting time and memory. The fourth wall generally remains intact, but the other three have not been inviolable.

Working within the frameworks of Ibsenian realism, expressionism, American thematic concerns, and their own creative processes, four of America's major playwrights—Eugene O'Neill, Thornton Wilder, Arthur Miller, and Tennessee Williams—have each used the drama to raise a different set of questions about the nature of the past and its relationship to the present. Each of them has also created a unique set of dramatic structures to explore the aspect of the past that most interests him.

Eugene O'Neill began these reforms by experimenting with both the concept and the techniques of exposition. In his early plays, O'Neill used antimimetic expository techniques to explore the characters' understanding of the past rather than to depict an objective sequence of preceding events. In his later plays, however, the characters become so obsessed with understanding the past that they are incapable of purposeful present action. In these plays a simple revision of expository techniques was no longer adequate, so O'Neill revised the entire sequence of traditional dramatic form, allowing exposition to subsume conflict, complication, and denouement.

For Thornton Wilder the problem was not one of exposing the past but rather of showing "two times at once": the "present" as characters perceive it and the "past" as history records it. This overlapping of temporal contexts is similar to that of the Elizabethans and so gave rise to a number of similarly self-conscious theatrical devices. Most obvious among them are the Stage Manager, who offers us multiple interpretations of the passing of time, and Wilder's parodies of nineteenth-century stage realism and its reductive vision of time.

Arthur Miller revised formal realism's concept of linear causality by placing "process" at the heart of each play. His notion of what "process" actually is, however, has evolved throughout his career. In his early plays, the process entails a character's revealing a causal secret from the past; these plays follow an appropriate Ibsenian retrospective method. In his later plays, the past causal moments are either unrecognized by the characters or (as in O'Neill's late plays) disputed among them. As a result, the characters must search through their memories to locate the events that have shaped their lives. This search through the past *becomes* the present action, and sequence becomes increasingly irrelevant to dramatic form.

Tennessee Williams's plays, like those of Wilder, present a double vision of time. In Williams's plays, time both passes in the present and remains frozen in the characters' memories. This double vision forms the basis for his characters' struggles and conflicts, as they attempt to control the present by controlling the accepted version of the past. It also became the locus for structural experiment: Williams typically depicted time present in traditional causal sequences, which are disrupted and sometimes obscured by the antimimetically depicted memories of his characters.

Each of these playwrights has built upon the structural innovations and resultant thematic variations of those who came before him, and each has developed his own unique dramatic style. What they have done in common, however, is place what was formerly thought of as "exposition" at the center of the present action rather than prior to it. As a result of this shift in conventional dramatic sequence, these playwrights have developed a characteristically American form of drama that is not, as Butcher predicted, "endlessly retrograde" but *is* repeatedly retrograde. This new American drama is uniquely able to explore a powerful, persistent, and expanding past that both influences and partially constitutes the perpetual stage present.

2

Eugene O'Neill
What the Past Has Made Them

For Eugene O'Neill, there was only one real subject for drama. As he remarked about *The Hairy Ape:*

> The subject here is the same ancient one that always was and always will be the one subject for drama, and that is man's struggle with his own fate. The struggle used to be with the gods, but it is now with himself, his own past. . . .[1]

Implicit in this statement are a number of the fundamental principles of O'Neill's entire career. Perhaps most obvious is the playwright's lifelong preoccupation with tragedy and its attendant focus on character rather than plot. But just as important, if less frequently discussed, is his emphasis on a past that never ceases to haunt his characters.

O'Neill's characters struggle with their pasts in virtually every one of his plays. Witness Smitty's "beastly memories" in *The Moon of the Caribbees*, Brutus Jones's frantic retreat from personal guilt and racial history in *The Emperor Jones*, Juan Ponce de Leon's compulsion to recover his lost youth in *The Fountain*, Nina Leeds's homage to the ghosts of her past in *Strange Interlude*, and the bums in Harry Hope's saloon, where "tomorrow is yesterday" in *The Iceman Cometh*, to name just a few. O'Neill's characters all seem to agree with Mary Tyrone in *Long Day's Journey into Night*, who claims that a person "can't help being what the past has made him."[2]

The notion of the past inherent in Mary Tyrone's statement and in many of O'Neill's plays, however, was not readily accessible to playwrights of the young O'Neill's generation. What the past makes of characters obviously depends on what those characters perceive the past to be. Likewise, that a character can "struggle" with his or her past suggests that the past is something open to question, changeable, and perhaps even unknowable. But as explained in chapter 1, the past as it invades the present or as individual characters interpret it had little currency on the formally realistic stage.

The American theatre with which O'Neill grew up was an arena for well-made plays and bombastic melodramas, characterized by complicated plotting, one-dimensional character types, and artfully contrived stage machinery. On this stage, the past comprised a series of anterior actions, appendages to the plot. But as O'Neill's remark about *The Hairy Ape* suggests, the young playwright was more interested in his characters' internal struggles than with formulaic plot construction. O'Neill insisted on assigning to character a dramatic priority that his recent predecessors had assigned to plot. As part of this refocusing of dramatic interests, O'Neill transplanted the past from the well-ordered rows of temporal events to the wilderness of his characters' minds. The past that produces so much present action in O'Neill's plays is rooted not only in causal incidents, but in the fluid and conflicting memories of his characters.

As a young playwright, then, O'Neill faced a dramaturgical problem. He saw that characters involved in internal struggles with the past would produce powerful drama. Yet he had inherited the prevailing stage conventions of his era, which offered numerous ways to complicate plot and to clarify anterior events but few techniques for exploring an unfixable and unfinished past. Because of this fundamental problem, O'Neill needed many years and varied dramatic experiments to coordinate his thematic interests with the structural innovations that would best enable him to portray them. The past is always important in an O'Neill play, but the nature of the past, its impact on the present, and especially the methods for dramatizing it vary throughout his career.

Much critical commentary on O'Neill's growth as a playwright has focused on the separate stages of his development, emphasizing his use of antimimetic devices and experimental forms early in his career and his return to a classically inspired naturalism in his later works.[3] But as Michael Selmon has warned, "we must beware of overemphasizing the distinctions between the phases of O'Neill's career. O'Neill's artistic development was essentially cumulative."[4] One important component shared by virtually all his plays is an unrelenting insistence on the past's complex and continuing influence. This concern, the matrix for O'Neill's growth into a major dramatist, appears as a theme in his early plays, as the aesthetic motivation for many of his experimental devices, and as theme, root of conflict, and source of action in his mature works.

O'Neill's late plays, which lack the sometimes obtrusive expository devices of his earlier works, are commonly regarded as his masterpieces. Yet the success of these plays derives less from O'Neill's abandoning his characteristic formal experiments than from his gradually unifying them with his characteristic theme of the remembered past's power. By the end of his career, O'Neill was able to eschew experimental devices because he had restructured the form of drama itself: he had revised the notion of "plot" by replacing conflict, climax, and resolution with an ongoing process of exposition. In his hands, exposition—what had formerly been a set of "not too improbable devices" for recounting past events—became, eventually, the very heart of dramatic action.

An examination of O'Neill's changing techniques will demonstrate how unified in aesthetic and thematic motivation his seemingly diverse experiments actually were. Virtually all of O'Neill's dramatic innovations, from technical devices to his ultimate restructuring of dramatic form, offered the playwright new options for dramatizing the past in the present time of the stage.

The One-Act Plays: Mood Made Audible

When a playwright working within the tradition of formal realism chooses to focus on character rather than plot, both the past germane to the play and the methods for including it in the present must change. Two possible solutions to this problem seem to have occurred to O'Neill early in his career. First, he began by writing one-act plays. Since action is necessarily limited in a short play, the form emphasizes character over plot; the past included in the play could therefore be the past that a character "struggles" with. Second, he experimented with the conventional devices of exposition, attempting to reveal the past through dramatic conflict—to embed it in the present—rather than to disclose it through an opening narration of facts. It would be decades before O'Neill would write full-length plays in which exposition of the past was the core of the drama, but his early one-act plays suggest his lifelong quest to revise the prevailing notion of the past and to include it in the apparently discrete stage present he had inherited.

The first O'Neill plays to be produced contain very little dramatic action of the usual kind. These plays concentrate instead on portraying a character's mood and suggesting the past events that provoked it. The best of these early one-acts anticipate the late plays by combining a character's memories or relics of the past with formal innovations that defy superficial realism. Gone, in the best one-acts, are the narrations of facts the characters already know; gone are the gossiping servants; gone are the confidants who disappear once they have outlived their dramatic usefulness. In their places are relatively complex characters whose stories and reminiscences arise directly from their dramatic situations. Since traditional plot, or the order of events, is of no special importance in these one-acts, their movement, like that of O'Neill's late plays, is backward in time (as Eugene Waith has described it),[5] a movement toward revelation or discovery for the characters.

The Moon of the Caribbees (1917) is among the best of these early plays in uniting the theme of memory with techniques that illustrate its power. The play takes place aboard the *S.S. Glencairn*, at anchor near a West Indian island. The focal point of the play is the character Smitty, who sits isolated by his potent memories. By the third line of the dialogue we learn, in a deft expository stroke, that Smitty's melancholy stems from a romantic attachment ("Down't be ser dawhn in the marf, Duke. She loves yer," Cocky tells him)[6] but it is left to Smitty himself, when the others have retreated below deck (offstage), to complain to the donkeyman about the "beastly memories" that haunt him night and day, estranging him from his shipmates and driving him to a solitary bottle of rum.

Since the play includes little "plot" of the conventional kind, O'Neill borrowed an expressionistic device to replace traditional exposition and suggest the "beastly memories" that Smitty can't shake off: "a melancholy Negro chant, faint and far off, drifts, crooning, over the water" (1:455). Smitty complains repeatedly about the song, claiming that "it makes you think of—well—things you ought to forget" (1:456). As it continues to carry over the moonlit water throughout the play, the song takes on added dramatic functions: it instigates Smitty's memories, provides a bit of West Indian background, and finally, by representing Smitty's state of mind, embodies the very mood it originally engendered. Like the beating tom-toms O'Neill would later use in *The Emperor Jones*, the native song with its implicit primitivism reveals the primal urgency of the things Smitty "ought to forget."

The mournful music, the delicate moonlight, and the physical distance between Smitty and his fellows all combine to create and sustain a meditative mood from beginning to end. What little action the play contains merely accents Smitty's isolation: he drinks alone; he rebuffs the native girls his companions pursue; he remains aloof from his mates' rowdy singing, drunken dancing, and inevitable fisticuffs. As he exits, *solus*, at the end of the play, the silence of the stage he leaves empty behind him is "broken only by the haunted, saddened voice of that brooding music, faint and far-off, like the mood of moonlight made audible" (1:474). Although Smitty never shares his memories with us, never interacts with his fellows nor reveals himself so completely as Hickey, the Tyrones, or even Con Melody will do in O'Neill's late plays, *The Moon of the Caribbees* succeeds in dramatizing the power of the past, as Smitty's undisclosed memories prove strong enough to prohibit him from acting in the present. In this play O'Neill takes a long step away from the one-dimensional characters and intricate plotting of what he called the "uninspired works of the Show Shop."[7] The playwright himself described *The Moon of the Caribbees* as his "first real break with theatrical tradition. Once I had taken this initial step, other plays followed logically."[8]

In *The Moon of the Caribbees* O'Neill portrayed the past as the dominant force in Smitty's present; the expressionistic song and the limited action both accent the theme of the remembered past. Smitty's melancholy memories reappear in *In the Zone* (1917), but this time his past is a catalyst for the actions of his crewmates as well as an important theme of the play. The *Glencairn* is now at sea, carrying ammunition through the dangerous war zone. When Smitty's crewmates, nervous about their mission, see him stealthily concealing a small box under his bunk, they accuse him of spying, beat him up, and break open the box, which contains nothing more sinister than some romantic letters from Smitty's now-lost love. Hylbert Opper has faulted this play for its Scribean contrivances—letters were, after all, a standard expository device of the well-made play—but the letters in *In the Zone* expose more than Smitty's prior love life. These letters, symbols of Smitty's history, arrest the action of the play and restore the focus of attention to Smitty and so to character, to mood, and to the enduring burden of a past that no plot reversals can change or eradicate. As the sailors rip open the box and read Smitty's letters, they reveal not only the source of Smitty's depression but also the paranoia brought on by the tensions of war and the destructiveness of their own suspicions; their actions reveal Smitty's past, its continuing control of his actions, and their own present terrors. This play anticipates the restructuring of dramatic form that O'Neill would undertake in the full-length plays of his maturity, in which uncovering the past both illuminates the past and constitutes the present.

In *Bound East for Cardiff* (1914), another *Glencairn* play focused on a character's recollections, the death of the sailor Yank is the only dramatic action. As in *The Moon of the Caribbees*, this diminution of plot indicates the extent to which O'Neill's abiding concern for the potency of the past generated structural changes in his plays. Early in the play the exposition of prior action is handled rather formulaically, as Davis simply narrates the story of Yank's injury. As Yank's death approaches, however, the play begins to resemble a lyric poem more than a formally realistic play. The prisonlike bunkroom setting, the dim cabin lighting, the foghorn blowing dismally outside, the oilskin-shrouded seamen, and the sleeping figures grouped around Yank combine to form an inarticulate sailor's elegy for the dying man. From this setting Yank's meditations on the past arise, a sort of deathbed confession. The expressionistic devices O'Neill here uses to evoke an elegiac mood combine with Yank's narrated memories to replace more conventional forms of action. Since the play moves backward in time, temporal sequence loses its priority to the mood of a character without a future—a character defined entirely by his remembered past.

In these three *Glencairn* plays, O'Neill's innovative devices and structural changes emphasized the remembered past and its continued invasion of the present. In a number of other one-act plays from this period, however, O'Neill was unable to embed the past so gracefully into the present. In *Where the Cross Is Made* (1918), for example—an otherwise interesting experiment in allowing the audience to share a character's mad visions—prior events are recited to a dramatically functionless character at the outset of the play, thereby diminishing the past to its former role of anterior action. *The Rope*

(1918) reduces the past even further, as Annie narrates her father's life story to him, tabulating demographic details he undoubtedly already knows about himself. O'Neill denied that the exposition in *The Rope* was awkward. His comment reveals his recurring interest in the past but also indicates his uncertainty, at this early point in his career, as to which methods of presenting a character's formative past were convincing, and even what type of past it was most useful to disclose. As he wrote to Nina Moise, who was directing the first production of *The Rope* in 1918:

> I don't agree with you about the exposition. It's dramatic exposition if ever I wrote any, and it's characterized, I flatter myself. . . . If the thing is acted naturally all that exposition will come right out of the characters themselves. . . . I see the exposition as a perfectly logical outcropping of the mood the different characters are in.[9]

These remarks show that even early in his career O'Neill was attempting to make the emergence of the past a logical consequence of a character's state of mind and of the present conflict. Although he perfected this technique decades later in *Long Day's Journey into Night*, in which the characters reveal the ongoing past gradually and continuously throughout the play, in *The Rope* he was unable to shake off the conventional massing of exposition at the outset of the play. In this play, as in many of his early efforts, O'Neill was unable to repair the radical separation of expository past and evolving present that he had inherited from formal realism.

Despite their occasional failings, these early plays suggest the recurring dramatic and structural problems with which O'Neill wrestled throughout his career, some of which he had already solved in the *Glencairn* plays. The problem remained, however, of incorporating such memory-bound characters and their internal struggles within full-length plays, which demanded more present action, more attention to plot. In his experimental full-length plays of the 1920s, O'Neill attacked the issue in a variety of ways: he tried to create psychologically complex characters, whose versions of the past could be changing and perhaps incompatible; he adapted classical and Ibsenian dramatic structures, both of which permit the past to emerge gradually, through character interaction, rather than through an opening recitation of facts; and he devised experimental expository devices to demonstrate the unverifiable nature of the past and its lingering impact on the present. If, seen in retrospect, these technical experiments sometimes distort O'Neill's focus on characters who must struggle with their pasts, it is because he himself was struggling to define exactly what the past entailed, how it mattered, and how one could best demonstrate its influence.

Full-Length Plays: Matters of Convention

With the Broadway premiere of *Beyond the Horizon* (written in 1918, produced in 1920) O'Neill achieved a triple success: his first full-length production, his first commercial hit, and his first play to disclose an ongoing past gradually, through character conflict rather than through mechanical expository devices (as in *The Rope*) or expressionistic ones (as in the *Glencairn* plays). The plot, based on the unwise decision of the wanderlustful Robert Mayo to remain on his family's farm while his landlubber brother Andrew takes his place at sea, does depend largely on traditional melodramatic action: the two brothers vie for Ruth's hand, their father disinherits the son who deserts him, a child dies, and a marriage disintegrates. But the play is notable in O'Neill's early work because simple dialogue becomes a primary expository device. For the first time the past is an integral component of present action, as the characters' refusal to forget directs them in the present.

Not surprisingly, the young O'Neill was not yet entirely in command of expository dialogue. Act 1 contains much conventional exposition, designed merely to inform the audience of prior events. The group discussions between the older Mayos and Mrs. Atkins tend to disrupt the dramatic action; the visiting Captain who needs to hear the news is transplanted directly from the well-made play; the long monologues of Robert and Ruth serve a primarily narrative function (although the past they discuss is at least subjective rather than known to both of them). But after this slow beginning O'Neill managed to incorporate quite a bit of exposition into the action.

In acts 2 and 3 the past becomes more a part of the present than a thing apart. As Robert and Ruth find it impossible to break a repeated cycle of conflicts, narration of the past gives way to dramatization of it. By continually digging up the past to reproach each other, the characters reveal the overlap between their past failures and their current problems. Through their quarrels the past comes alive on the stage, reenacted endlessly in the present.

The past's continuing hold on the present is depicted by the setting of the play as well as by the dialogue. As the acts change and time passes between them, the decor of the Mayo farm interior degenerates from homely comfort in act 1 to disorder and disrepair in act 2 to absolute poverty, reflecting despair, in act 3. Before the characters even speak in each act, the set itself tells us something of the ruination of the farm, of the birth of a child (whose toys suddenly litter the stage), of Robert's unwillingness to leave his books and his daydreams behind him, and of Ruth's inability to manage an orderly household. The set itself becomes an expository device.

Even more significant than O'Neill's use of conflict and setting to reveal the past is a technique he used for the first time in *Beyond the Horizon* and would use again and again, with varying degrees of success: long intervals of time (three and five years, respectively) elapsing offstage between acts. This technique was evidently an attempt to dramatize the events that influence each succeeding act, and so avoid both the narrated expositions of some of his early one-acts and the elaborately mechanical plotting of conventional realism. In *Beyond the Horizon* the passage of so much offstage time works well after the first act, which, as explained earlier, still relies on monologues and long-lost relatives. The second and third acts, however, are more like O'Neill's one-act plays: each depicts a climactic moment set in motion by prior choices. Unlike the choices in the one-acts, however, the Mayos' choices are made onstage in act 1 and enacted before us, so we are privy to two sorts of pasts: the factual past of anterior events and the changing, recollected past that the characters make use of in the present. For the first time in an O'Neill play, the playwright shows us that the past varies as it is carried into the present. Preceding events are, in fact, a very small part of what the influential past entails.

While allowing long passages of time to pass between acts was probably a major breakthrough for a young dramatist attempting to make the transition from one-act to full-length plays, the device created problems of its own in some of O'Neill's early full-length works. A case in point is *Diff'rent* (1920), in which the two acts of the play embrace a thirty-year interval, the longest in O'Neill's canon. The play is structurally similar to *Beyond the Horizon* in that a misguided decision made in act 1 (in this case, Emma's breaking her engagement to Caleb) is shown to have disastrous repercussions in act 2, by which time Emma's romantic idealism has withered into neurotic sexuality, and Caleb's dogged but unrewarded devotion finally drives him to suicide. The play also resembles *Beyond the Horizon* in the visually effective changes in set and costume that demonstrate Emma's rejection of her past.

Despite the similarity of technique to *Beyond the Horizon*, however, and the interesting study of sexual repression that the play presents, *Diff'rent* exposes many of the weaknesses inherent in the use of long between-act intervals. Continuity of character becomes nearly impossible when thirty years of unrecorded time elapse between acts, as William Jennings Adams has noted.[10] And as John Henry Raleigh has argued, O'Neill's plays that cover huge stretches of time typically depend on melodramatic situations (such as a gestation period or the growth of a character) which necessitate the gap in dramatic action.[11] In *Diff'rent* the problem is exaggerated even further by two factors: the lack of psychological complexity in the characters and the indisputable, linear connection between past and present. Unlike the Mayos of *Beyond the Horizon*, whose self-analyses lead to conflict, revelation, and awareness, Emma's self-realization stems not from any trait or activity of her own, but from the brutal frankness of the profligate Benny—a device of the plot. And because her change in character (both between acts and again after Benny's cruelty) is abrupt rather than gradual, the only notion of the past that the play can depict is the simplified one of sequential, causal events. In this play O'Neill avoided conventional expository devices but failed to revise the conventional notions of what the past entails or how it intrudes into the present.

In *Gold* (1920), a four-act play, O'Neill once again used a substantial length of time between the first two acts. The play exposes the most serious of the technical problems that plagued O'Neill's efforts to replace formulaic expository scenes with long between-act intervals. The first act depicts some members of a shipwrecked crew stranded on a desert island, crazed with heat and thirst, who murder two of their crewmates in a deranged controversy over some cheap trinkets they believe to be gold. This is the past mistake that, like Robert's deciding to remain on the farm and Emma's breaking her engagement, precipitates the action of the later acts (which take place six months later) and initiates Captain Bartlett's guilty madness. Because the last three acts take place in a different setting and among a host of characters not present in act 1, however, the exposition of anterior action takes the conventional form of a recitation of events. As Heywood Broun, a contemporary reviewer, saw it, after the first act "exposition sets in most malignantly":

> The exigencies of the plot require that the captain shall tell of the finding of the treasure and the murder of the two crew members again and again. Nor is there the usual excuse that such long discursive interludes are put in as a favor to the audience. This time the audience knows and does not need to be told.[12]

But a problem even more difficult than tiresome expository narratives emerges from this technique of presenting a significant past event as it happens: the past is thus presented as an incontrovertible series of incidents rather than as a complex of forces, both inner and outer, shaping the characters' destinies. We have seen the murder of the crewmates, and we know that the treasure is only brass. By allowing the audience to witness the formative past, O'Neill objectifies the incidents as they occur and loses the focus on characters and their perceptions that he had begun so painstakingly to develop in his one-act plays. Captain Bartlett's guilt may confuse his family and drive him mad, but the audience is not permitted to share in the emotional reality of the characters' uncertainty. And unlike the past portrayed in *Beyond the Horizon*, the past of *Gold*'s act 1 is neither shared by the principal characters of subsequent acts nor remembered variously by them. The ambiguities of the past are thus reduced to a set of verifiable facts, and the events as witnessed, not the variety of the characters' recollections nor the possible repercussions, remain uppermost in our minds.

Although O'Neill continued to write plays with lengthy between-act intervals, he must have recognized the uneasy trade-off he achieved with this technique: he emphasized the power of the past to influence the present by depicting it all on the stage, but he lost the focus on characters' interior realities—including their idiosyncratic uses of the past—that he had hoped to develop. These plays thus became progressively more experimental throughout O'Neill's career, as he strove to allow revelation of the characters' memories to arise directly from them. His famous masks (used most notably in *The Great God Brown*, 1925, and *Lazarus Laughed*, 1926) are the most obvious example. O'Neill used masks to illustrate, among other things, the characters' inability to come to terms with their true emotions or their memories, and their consequent rejection of responsibility for present actions. According to O'Neill's "Memoranda on Masks," the use of masks solved the problem of expressing "those profound hidden conflicts of the mind which the probings of psychology continue to disclose to us."[13]

Although masks allowed O'Neill to dramatize aspects of his characters that they themselves are often unwilling to acknowledge, the masks turned out to be visually distracting. Moreover, too often the burden of a character's struggle for self-awareness is carried by a change of mask (an exterior device) instead of by a revealing self-disclosure or through present conflict.

If O'Neill's reviving of masks had only a limited usefulness in emphasizing the presence of the past, he succeeded better with the aside, a technique that allowed his characters to discover their own inner truths, probe their memories, and reveal those truths and memories for themselves. *Strange Interlude* (1927), although in some ways as contrived as the masking plays, demonstrates the value of the aside and soliloquy in a modern context and succeeds in ways the other experimental plays do not. The play clearly demonstrates O'Neill's continuing interest in self-revealing characters and forcefully examines the role of the ongoing past in determining their present actions.

Strange Interlude is a monolithic play, stretching over twenty-five years of stage time in nine acts and almost five hours of audience time. The asides and soliloquies that form so much of the script provide a unique and workable method for exposing characters, examining their motives, exploring their memories, and sounding their unspoken emotional responses to events. As O'Neill defended the technique against its detractors:

> Everything is a matter of convention. If we accept one, why not another, so long as it does what it's intended to do? My people speak aloud what they think and what the others aren't supposed to hear.[14]

The trouble with the asides in *Strange Interlude* is that they don't always do what O'Neill here suggests they were "intended to do." While many of the speeches do reveal the inner secrets of the characters and their conflicting versions of their mutual past, a great many others (Lawson estimates ninety percent)[15] deal with trivialities or with secrets the characters reveal anyway in the ensuing dialogue. In act 5, for example, Nina and Ned spend several pages ruminating in asides about their secret love for each other, just before they proclaim it through dialogue. The asides here provide a good technique for generating suspense, perhaps, but hardly the exposition of souls O'Neill claimed to be striving for. And many characters end up repeating the banalities of conversation in their asides, with little cause and little new information to impart.

The title of the play is taken from one of Nina's more revealing asides, in which she ponders her present indifference to the man who was once her all-consuming love. She says to herself:

> The only living life is in the past and future . . . the present is an interlude . . . strange interlude in which we call on past and future to bear witness we are living! (1 : 165; ellipsis O'Neill's)

For Nina, life is expectation and memory. O'Neill therefore chose to present only the climactic moments of her life, the ones that her anticipation colors and her memory retains; he directs our attention, like Nina's, to the events that partially determine the future. To his credit, O'Neill managed to capture a moment of crisis, the convergence of past incidents and present emotion, in almost every scene (as he had done in *Beyond the Horizon*). In act 1, for instance, Nina resents her father's meddling in her career plans. The ensuing argument rekindles her resentment of his previous meddling in her love affair with Gordon and reveals her guilty feelings about that love.

The success of presenting even the crucial events of a twenty-five-year era, however, is mixed. Despite the genuine skill with which O'Neill was now using present conflict to reveal the past gradually, depicting the passage of decades produces problems—apparent in most of the plays of long stage duration—that O'Neill was as yet unable to solve. As in *Gold*, when each scene is enacted before the audience, the shaping past is reduced to an irrefutable set of facts; the objective record of events overshadows the remembered past that motivates the characters in the present. And when the past remains thus frozen for the audience, exposition takes the form of unnecessary repetition instead of a dynamic expression of unique memories. In *Strange Interlude*, O'Neill managed to avoid much of this tedium by building each act around a character's crisis and the resulting revelations, but occasionally "exposition sets in most malignantly" again as one character or another needs to be brought up to date on the events he or she has missed. Act 4 provides a particularly painful example of such mechanical exposition, as Nina informs Darrell of all that took place while he was offstage in act 3. Apparently the problem of repeating what the audience has already witnessed is an almost insurmountable stumbling block in a play that dramatizes the passage of decades while simultaneously exploring the continuing influence of the past.

The plays that depict long time spans (either enacted or occurring between acts) allowed O'Neill to portray one kind of past—the outwardly visible chain of events—at the cost of continuity and gradual character development. But for a playwright so involved in developing psychologically complete stage people, the inner past of memory and interpretation begged to be expressed more fully. In plays depicting a briefer time period, O'Neill found ways to expose this inner past without a break in the dramatic action. *The Emperor Jones* (1920) is the first success of this sort and a crucial step in the development of O'Neill's dramatic skills. In its adherence to the classical unities of time, place, and action, the play anticipates O'Neill's great last plays.[16] But *The Emperor Jones* is a major accomplishment in its own right, for in it O'Neill combined an unfixed and partially unrecognized version of the past with experimental techniques well designed to explore its impact.

The only major actor of the play is the Emperor Brutus Jones, and the only significant action is his attempted escape from his rebellious subjects during the course of one evening. The eight scenes of the play follow each other in rapid succession, with hours rather than years elapsing between them. As Jones, lost in the dark, travels full circle through the primeval forest and ends up, at daybreak, exactly where he began, his fears and memories, embodied on the stage, also travel through a full circle of personal and racial history. *The Emperor Jones* is thus the first of O'Neill's plays (to be followed more than a decade later by *Mourning Becomes Electra* and *Long Day's Journey into Night*) to use exposition as the central action and so become cyclic in structure: the lack of present action other than that which reveals the past prevents the play from moving forward.

The first scene of the play is expository in a mechanical way, as Jones and his cohort Smitty describe both the Emperor's present dangers and his history—including his knifing of a gambling opponent and his subsequent murder of a chain gang guard. But as the natives offstage begin beating their sinister tom-toms and darkness falls in the forest through which Jones tries to escape, the objective facts of Jones's past become less important than the panic that triggers his memories. As the steady pulsating of the drums accelerates in imitation of Jones's pounding heartbeat, his fears give rise to hallucinations in which he relives the past he and Smitty have already recounted. This time, however, the audience witnesses not simply the outer events of Brutus Jones's life, but his own personal and perhaps distorted recollection of them. We learn, for instance, that he never intended to murder the gambler, and that his escape from the chain gang was not planned but spontaneous, triggered by anger. Furthermore, as terror strips away layer after layer of Jones's cherished veneer of civilization, his personal memories of murder and escape give way to a flood of subconscious racial fears and primal instincts. The slave auction, the Congo Witch Doctor, and the Crocodile God all appear to belie Jones's claim to be beyond superstition; they expose an inner reality that Jones himself would hardly recognize, let alone express. [17]

Herein lies the importance of *The Emperor Jones:* since the play reveals Jones's response to the inescapable past rather than an objective series of events, the audience can share the experience of his fearful memories. We are no longer witnesses to an action but participants in an emotional reality, as Jones's deepest terrors appear in the flesh, on the stage before us. Even more significant is the vision of the shaping past that the play presents. Unlike *Beyond the Horizon, Gold,* or *Diff'rent,* in which a single ill-conceived decision forever alters the lives of the characters, *The Emperor Jones* presents the past as a complex and penetrating force, in part formed by a character's choices but largely beyond his control and partly beyond the limits of his understanding. In this early play O'Neill managed to construct a past with implications far more profound than those of the Scribean pasts his lavishly mounted experimental plays sometimes depended on.

In *The Emperor Jones* O'Neill thus discovered which sort of past is most useful in developing complex characters. Despite his subsequent deviations from this model, it came to have lasting consequences later in his career. The play itself does have weaknesses, however, particularly in character development—weaknesses that for a time seem to have led O'Neill away from his focus on the remembered past. We do come to know Brutus Jones intimately, but our knowledge comes from O'Neill's virtuoso handling of expressionistic devices—his objectification of Jones's emotional state—rather than through character interaction or any new self-awareness on Jones's part. It seems that even in the best of O'Neill's experimental plays he managed to hit only one of his twin targets: either the past, inescapable and overwhelming, persists in affecting the characters without extending their knowledge (as in *The Emperor Jones*); or the characters explore their interior lives through interaction, which leads them to understand themselves but not the past (as in *Strange Interlude*). One is tempted to agree with Eric Bentley's assessment (and O'Neill's eventual understanding) that O'Neill's "ambition to transcend realism" only muddled up his plays.[18] It was not until O'Neill abandoned his nonrealistic methods of revelation—his masks, asides, soliloquies, and expressionistic devices—that his characters finally begin to reveal both their inner realities and their own emerging and mutable visions of the past.

Dramatic Maturity: Let Them Reveal Themselves

In writing his numerous versions of *Mourning Becomes Electra* (1931), O'Neill recapitulated his entire dramatic career. His first draft included asides; another, soliloquies; a later one, masks. But when O'Neill finally relinquished this experimental mannerism and decided to portray the conflicts of the Mannon family in a simpler, more classical style, he hit upon a nearly perfect method for dramatizing the continuing presence of the past. In his working diary O'Neill recorded his decision to eschew experimental devices in the trilogy:

> Job now is to get all this in naturally in straight dialogue—as simple and direct and dynamic as possible—with as few words—stop doing things to these characters—let them reveal themselves.[19]

What O'Neill had formerly expressed with experimental dramatic devices he now left up to his characters, whose grapplings with the past thus become more immediate, more intense, and more central to the drama. The trilogy in effect internalizes exposition, which becomes the work's central process rather than a set of devices grafted onto the action. With this shift in dramatic emphasis, O'Neill was finally able to dramatize an internally constructed, unverifiable past that is inseparable from the present.

The past intrinsic to *Mourning Becomes Electra* exerts a much more complex influence than the more orderly past that determined the fates of the Mayo brothers or Nina Leeds. Orin and Lavinia Mannon never make the one simple mistake that forever haunts so many of O'Neill's characters. Rather, they are doomed to reenact the very crimes of their forebears that they originally set out to avenge; like that of the Emperor Jones, their seemingly forward progress turns out to be an endless circling back. Lavinia's unbending judgments of Christine, her mother, illustrate the process. Disgusted at Christine's adultery, Lavinia incites Orin to murder Brant (their mother's lover), and she herself drives Christine to suicide. When Lavinia later discovers on her South Seas voyage that "everything about love can be sweet and natural" (2:154), however, and when she learns that Brant was, in fact, justified in seeking revenge on the Mannon family for their casting out his parents (also victims of "illicit" love), Lavinia's guilt expands to include all the family crimes she has unwittingly repeated. Orin recognizes his sister's involvement in the inherited pattern: "So many strange things out of the Mannon past combine in you!" he tells her (2:153). The past thus comes alive—for characters and for audience—by being reenacted in the present.

The complexity of the past's hold on the present is further compounded by Orin's and Lavinia's idiosyncratic and changing perspectives on it. What Orin sees as a long record of family crimes Lavinia at first sees as "only justice" (2:165); the differences in their viewpoints and the eventual change in Lavinia's outlook require constant readjustments of our own interpretation of the past. Only one thing about this unfixed, subjective past is certain, and that is its continual power over present and future. Even the characters recognize the intricate threads of the past tangled in their lives. As Orin tells his sister:

> I've tried to trace to its secret hiding place in the Mannon past the evil destiny behind our lives! I thought if I could see it clearly in the past I might be able to foretell what fate is in store for us. (2:153)

The stage presentation of this cyclic, recurring past is necessarily very different from that of the more linear, sequential pasts of some of O'Neill's earlier plays, although each play of the trilogy does begin with a massing of exposition as Seth the gardener relates the ancient Mannon history to his cronies. O'Neill evidently considered the gardener a form of Greek chorus—"a human background for the drama of the Mannons" (2:67)—but these minor characters who disappear after the first act of each play look suspiciously like Scribean servants. In this case, however, the convention has been put to an innovative use: the anterior action revealed by these townsfolk provides a publicly accepted version of the past to contrast with Orin and Lavinia's re-creation of it. But unlike the historical past revealed in the early acts of such plays as *Diff'rent* and *Gold*, this past is never enacted before us. Seth and his cohorts reveal only their own version of what has gone before.

The more complex, unnarratable, continually recurring past is revealed not through such devices, however, but through the present conflicts of the characters. O'Neill had used this technique to a limited extent as early as *Beyond the Horizon*, but he developed it more completely in the trilogy so that the characters could discover and "reveal themselves." Particularly in *The Homecoming* and *The Haunted* (the first and third plays of the trilogy), the intense relationships among the characters elicit the disclosures of their past secrets and provoke their reinterpretations of the shaping past. In *The Homecoming*, for example, Lavinia's jealous taunts at Brant provoke him to tell her the story of his birth, but the tale he tells of the Mannons' rejecting his parents is not the story Lavinia expected to hear. As she denies Brant's charge of Mannon perfidy, her plans for revenge harden into firm resolve. Character interaction thereby induces revelation of the past, and the revelation in turn generates further dramatic conflict.

This cyclic pattern of truth revealed in moments of intense emotion is repeated endlessly throughout the trilogy, as Lavinia incites Christine to disclose the truth about her affair, Christine forces her husband to a new understanding of their entangled relationship, and Orin, provoked by guilt and his sister's jibes, faces his ghosts with a bullet through his brain. As O'Neill wrote to George Jean Nathan about the violent emotions of his trilogy:

> There are plays of direct passion and intensity, and involved, inhibited cerebrations don't belong in them. I monkeyed around with schemes for dialogue and ideas for production until my head ached—but the story I had to tell made all such stuff seem futile and I finally settled down to the direct and least noticeable way, and I find I can get everything said about these characters' souls, hearts, and loins that can be said.[20]

In *Mourning Becomes Electra*, character confrontation leads to revelation of the hidden past, which leads back to character confrontation.

This recurring movement allowed O'Neill to fuse his twin preoccupations; the persistent past and the emotional reality of the characters could both emerge in a never-ending cycle of past and present that replaced simple linear causality. He was finally able to relinquish his obtrusive experimental devices because he had restructured realistic dramatic form.

The internalization of device in *Mourning Becomes Electra* was a major step forward—perhaps *the* major step—in the increasing intertwining of theme and technique that marks O'Neill's career. One on level, however, the trilogy still depends on conventional stage trappings to an extraordinary degree, although the conventions are classical rather than formally realistic or experimental. The chorus of townspeople; the Aristotelian handling of time, location, and action; the use of dramatic irony; the three-part structure; and the story itself: these are all successful transplants from the Greek original, and all apparent at the start, as the title of the trilogy indicates. Even O'Neill's additions to the ancient story—such as the incest motive for Orin and Lavinia, the suicide of Orin, and the cursed house—harmonize with the standard Greek themes and devices (as Stark Young has noted).[21] The final step O'Neill was to take in revising dramatic form was a further elimination of obvious conventions, regardless of their source. In *The Iceman Cometh* (1939), *Long Day's Journey into Night* (1941), and *A Moon for the Misbegotten* (1943), O'Neill embedded principles of Greek tragedy within otherwise naturalistic plays and so fully realized his lifelong goal of dramatizing "man and his struggle with . . . himself, his own past." In these plays it is, indeed, the "struggle" to understand the formative past that shapes the present action.

The retrospective action of O'Neill's late plays has been described in various ways. For Waith, it is "a movement toward unmasking"; for Rudolf Stamm, an impulse toward confession and rebirth; for Raleigh, a transference of the "necessary machinery at the beginning of the play" to "the entire substance of the play itself."[22] But the real success of these plays lies in O'Neill's ability to combine the notion of a persistent yet manipulable past with the technical skill necessary to produce the plays' retrograde movement.

The achievement of the late naturalistic plays becomes sharply apparent if we contrast them with O'Neill's historical play on the same theme written during the same period, 1935–42. In *A Touch of the Poet*, Con Melody has invented the past of an Irish nobleman for himself.

When he is finally forced to recognize his dream past as fiction, his self-made splendor collapses, the "bogtrotter" Irishman reappears, and he realizes that he has "no future but the past."[23] The major weakness of the play stems from the nature of Melody's memories: although his version of the shaping past is subjective, the audience is offered a fixed, factual version of the past by his long-suffering wife, his daughter, and other, minor characters. The past is thus once again reduced to a series of verifiable anterior actions, and exposition depends on the mechanical devices that reveal it. But while the play suffers from a number of structural flaws, it is important for two reasons: first, because the intense emotional conflicts that generate revelation (especially the midnight confessional scene between Sara and Nora) are among the most moving and effective in O'Neill's canon; and second, because the structure of the play indicates the direction and ultimate achievement of O'Neill's last plays. As Henry Hewes noted in his review of the original production:

> If *A Touch of the Poet* suffers somewhat from over-exposition, too many vital scenes occurring offstage, and a plethora of old-fashioned melodramatic plot details, it at the same time foreshadows O'Neill's growth into his final great period. . . . He seems to be saying "Here's your damned exposition and climaxes. They are arbitrary and unreal. The true drama lies in the moments of anguish and love!"[24]

No play of O'Neill's dramatizes those "moments of anguish and love" better than *Long Day's Journey into Night*, although *The Iceman Cometh* and *A Moon for the Misbegotten* share many of its most effective dramatic components. In all three plays O'Neill observes the unities of time, place, and action, and this formal structure, in combination with his focus on character and the priority he assigns to memory, delivers the concentrated emotional power of the plays.[25] In all three plays the action is largely retrospective, and the plays all contrast a dynamic and continually influential past with a present devoid of possibilities. As several critics have noted, each play depends in large part on the device of alcohol consumption: as the characters get increasingly intoxicated throughout the play their inhibitions are lowered, nostalgia sets in, and they reveal their own concepts of their innermost selves.[26] Each play moves in a cycle from dawn to deepest night (and, in *Iceman* and *Moon*, back again), from comedy to tragedy, from hope to despair.[27] In short, each play proceeds as the characters in it struggle to confront the past, whether by denial of responsibility for it (the Tyrones, Larry Slade), reconstruction of it (the bums at Harry Hope's saloon), or confession of it (Jamie Tyrone, the misbegotten). If *Long Day's Journey* is the best of the three—and I think it is—its superiority comes from its unrelenting focus on a small group of interlocking characters (unlike the more diffuse *Iceman*) and on a single effect (unlike the rather abrupt shift of focal character and mood in *Moon*).

Only two significant events take place on the day in 1912 depicted in *Long Day's Journey into Night*, and both of them happen offstage: Edmund Tyrone discovers that he has tuberculosis, and Mary Tyrone resumes her dependency on drugs. The degree to which the past is central to this play can be seen by the retroactive chain of events that links these two central facts together. Mary first became addicted to drugs at Edmund's birth twenty-three years before the play begins; she returns to drugs in 1912 because she fears that Edmund has inherited his tuberculosis from her. To help alleviate her guilt, Mary blames her addiction on all the other members of her family. She blames Tyrone for miserliness in hiring a cheap doctor at Edmund's birth and also for wanting a child (Edmund) to replace a baby who had died; she blames that baby's death on Jamie; and she blames Edmund himself, whose difficult birth precipitated her addiction in the first place. Each of the four Tyrones lives thus imprisoned by a similar chain of guilt and blame forged by each of their memories, and their never-ending accusations and recriminations about the past dominate them in the present. What little action takes place on the stage revolves around this struggle with the past.

Like *Mourning Becomes Electra*, which records a continuing cycle of family history, the action of *Long Day's Journey* grows out of its own cycle of confrontations, as each character's feelings of guilt for the family misery collide with his or her need to place blame elsewhere. Each confrontation leads to a revelation about the past, and each revelation leads to another confrontation. The middle section of act 1 illustrates this cyclic process. As Edmund leaves the room in disgust after quarreling with his father, the following speeches ensue: Jamie asserts that Edmund is seriously ill, which Tyrone denies; Tyrone cites Dr. Hardy, whose opinion Mary disparages; Tyrone berates Jamie for upsetting his mother, and Jamie accuses Tyrone of miserliness; Tyrone sneers at Jamie's failure as an actor, and Jamie mocks Tyrone's theatrical pretensions; Tyrone accuses Jamie of contributing to Edmund's ill health, which Jamie denies; Jamie remarks that Mary seems particularly nervous, which Tyrone first denies but later confirms; and finally Jamie and Tyrone attribute Mary's condition to, successively, Edmund's illness, Edmund's birth, cheap physicians, and the miserly Tyrone. Within ten pages of first-act dialogue we learn the history of the Tyrone family, the dynamics of their present relationships, and the extent to which they are currently imprisoned by their constant exploitation of the past.

Thus far, the play seems to resemble earlier O'Neill works, like *Beyond the Horizon* or *Mourning Becomes Electra*, in which character interaction and conflict are used as expository devices. In *Long Day's Journey*, however, expository action reaches a new level of importance, as dealing with the past and its present repercussions becomes the sole activity of the characters. As O'Neill himself described the play, it is:

> the story of one day, 8 A.M. to midnight, in the life of a family of four—father, mother and two sons—back in 1912,—a day in which things occur which evoke the whole past of the family and reveal every aspect of its interrelationships. A deeply tragic play, but without any violent dramatic action. At the final curtain, there they still are, trapped within each other by the past, each guilty and at the same time innocent, scorning, loving, pitying each other, understanding and yet not understanding at all, forgiving but still doomed never to be able to forget.[28]

In the Tyrones' world of repeated accusations and recriminations, the conventional plot sequence of exposition, complication, climax, and resolution dissolves. There is no ordering to the Tyrones' memories other than the logic of association; the syntax of their memories allows them to create causality at will and so evade responsibility for the past they are "doomed never to forget." It is therefore fitting that this play avoids beginning with conventional exposition and ends by refusing to conclude; the cyclic structure of the play reflects the endlessly retrograde nature of the characters' quarrels. The curtain falls on the four tormented Tyrones still locked within the circles of their memories, unable to locate themselves in a mutually agreeable plot sequence that would permit them to confront the past and future. Mary's belief that "the past is the present, isn't it? It's the future, too" (87) is manifest in the play's open-ended structure, which includes no introductory exposition, no conventional dramatic action, and no possible resolution.

In the absence of sequential plot movement, the words spoken by the characters are all that remain to structure the play. These speeches, in fact, reveal the extent to which O'Neill had revised dramatic structure to center on the past. Instead of beginning with an informative monologue or with two minor characters gossiping, act 1, as we have seen, plunges us immediately into the quarrels, based on conflicting versions of the past, that form the Tyrones' present lives—the actual action of the play. In act 4, when a conventional well-made play would reach the climax of the action, *Long Day's Journey* halts for prolonged expository monologues. With the foghorn blowing eerily outside and Mary's drugged footsteps dragging overhead, the three Tyrone men, all drunk, take turns quarreling and then reconciling by means of long stories from their formative pasts. Tyrone describes his impoverished childhood and artisitic frustrations to explain away his niggardliness; Edmund uses his feelings of unity with the sea to explain his fascination with death; and Jamie confesses in drunken anguish the childhood events that led him to corrupt his brother. By replacing conventional action with exposition, O'Neill inserted the past—inconclusive yet insurmountable—at the very center of the drama.

In one sense, the real "action" of the play takes place in the audience: we are constantly forced to alter our vision of the Tyrones' past, since the characters embellish or contradict each others' stories in virtually every line of dialogue. Mary's version of her father's comfortable home and of her longing to join a convent, for example, is the truth as Mary remembers it and as we first know it; but Tyrone's interpretation of her middle-class home as ordinary and his decription of the young Mary as "a bit of a rogue and a coquette, God bless her" (138) cast suspicion on Mary's memories, on our understanding of the past, and on the credibility of both characters. This cycle of continual reinterpretation through dialogue portrays the past as changeable, continually influential, and never fully knowable, and forces us into the fog of subjective truths and disputed memories that hovers over the seemingly hopeless present of the Tyrones. In *Long Day's Journey into Night* O'Neill not only challenged the distinction between past and present, he also broke down the barrier between stage and spectator that had been erected along with the proscenium arch.

The Past Which Is Never the Past

O'Neill's importance to the American theatre has long been recognized; he was, after all, our first major playwright, our first creative dramatist of lasting impact and significant achievement. I have emphasized only two of his accomplishments because they determined the shape of his entire career: first, his continuing interest in expanding the conventional notion of the stage past, and second, his resultant attention to reshaping dramatic form. O'Neill's comment on what he hoped to achieve in *Anna Christie* applies equally well to the development of his whole career:

> I wanted to have the audience leave with a deep feeling of life flowing on, of the past which is never the past—but always the birth of the future—of a problem solved for the moment but by the very nature of its solution involving new problems.[29]

Like so many of his characters, O'Neill as a playwright repeatedly faced problems that he could solve only provisionally, play by play, and that therefore required constant innovation. His revolt against plot-centered melodrama, his interest in characters who interact and develop, his experiments with antimimetic expository devices, and his ultimate revision of traditional dramatic sequence all enabled him, eventually, to depict a past that includes more than anterior events and affects the present in pervasive and profound ways.

O'Neill's influence on the American playwrights who came after him has also been pervasive and profound. Through his experiments and achievements, O'Neill opened up the proscenium stage to areas of human experience not previously accessible to it. While this widening of theatrical horizons may have produced a dramatic problem for his successors that "by the very nature of its solution [involves] new problems," he also empowered them to explore a past that is not necessarily factual, sequential, or agreed-upon, and to portray its connections to the present in diverse and meaningful ways. As subsequent chapters will demonstrate, the American dramatists who succeeded O'Neill took advantage of his work in unique ways. Some chose to explore alternative versions of the past; some chose to experiment with devices of exposition; some have adapted his open-ended dramatic form, where exposition becomes a process rather than a first-act device. What they have all taken from O'Neill, however, is the interest in and ability to explore a powerful, persistent, and unfixable past within the once rigidly bounded world of formal realism.

3

Thornton Wilder
Disparate Moments and Repetitive Patterns

At first glance, Thornton Wilder's stage past may seem to have only a tenuous connection with that of other twentieth-century American playwrights. For O'Neill, Miller, and Williams, the past is present in the memories of the characters; exposition therefore assumes a major dramatic role in their plays. Yet Wilder's work does share his compatriots' concern with portraying time's passage on the stage, although his emphasis is somewhat different. On Wilder's stage, time's passing is most often obvious to us but unnoticed by the characters, even as it shapes their lives and changes the world they inhabit.

In a 1956 essay entitled "The Man Who Abolished Time," Malcolm Cowley pointed out Wilder's pervasive interest in the effects of time. According to Cowley, Wilder's guiding principle and recurring theme is that *"Everything that happened might happen anywhere and will happen again."*[1] As a result of this principle, says Cowley, Wilder continually experiments with time in his novels and his plays, "foreshortening time" to emphasize the repeated patterns of history. Cowley's essay is a landmark, since it offers one of the first analyses of Wilder's perennial experiments with time. Yet Cowley's assessment (both in the 1956 article and in an expanded version published in 1973) is somewhat misleading, suggesting that Wilder holds a "disregard for history" and even that he "denies the importance of time."[2]

It would be more accurate to say that Wilder's *characters* deny the importance of time; they do their best to preserve inherited patterns—annual Christmas dinners, familiar wedding ceremonies—designed to stave off the changes that time inevitably, if imperceptibly, brings with it. Yet to the spectators of a Wilder play, time passes quickly and visibly: characters grow gray before our eyes, and the Ice Age is immediately followed by World War II. With the exception of some very early plays, time is rarely "abolished" on Wilder's stage; rather, it becomes an actual theatrical presence.

This difference between time as it passes and time as characters perceive it is at the heart of Wilder's dramatic experiments; one might even call it the central conflict of his plays. For Wilder was aware that time passes at different rates, depending on who is measuring the pace. For a geologist, centuries count as nothing; for an archeologist or a historian, time collapses; for a lover in the presence of the beloved, an hour can pass unnoticed, yet to one who must wait, that same hour can seem interminable. Rather than focusing his theatrical experiments on methods of exposition, then, Wilder concentrated on depicting the profound and inescapable effects of time as well as the many perspectives available to measure its passing.

Throughout his career Wilder devised, recovered, and adapted stage techniques that produce a double vision of past and present, that demonstrate the role of the individual moment in creating the repeated patterns of history. The playwright described his problem in this way:

Every person who has ever lived has lived an unbroken succession of unique occasions. Yet the more one is aware of individuality in experience (innumerable! innumerable!) the more one becomes attentive to what these disparate moments have in common, to repetitive patterns. As an artist (or listener or beholder) which "truth" do you prefer—that of the isolated occasion, or that which includes or resumes the innumerable? Which truth is more worth telling?[3]

Wilder's plays suggest that he found *both* truths worth telling, and his dramatic experiments all contribute to his expressing them simultaneously. He continually adjusted stage time to portray situations both as "disparate moments" and also as contributors to "repetitive patterns." By presenting, as he said of *The Skin of Our Teeth*, "two times at once,"[4] he was able to proclaim the intrinsic significance of each moment and simultaneously to explore the place of the moment, once past, in shaping the unfolding patterns of history.

The Compression of Time

Wilder's very first published plays (*The Angel That Troubled the Waters*, 1928) suggest both his willingness to experiment with stage time and the early difficulties he faced in creating a temporally flexible dramatic form; many of these plays, in fact, do "abolish" time in just the way Cowley described. The form the young Wilder employed—and Wilder admits to having begun experimenting with these plays while still a high school student—was the three-minute play for three actors, a literary form that, according to the playwright's "Forward" to the volume, "satisfies my desire for compression."[5] Despite the immaturity of the three-minute plays themselves, this impulse toward compression led the young Wilder to experiment with the telescoping of time, thereby allowing his three minutes of stage time to incorporate many of the general patterns of history. The three-minute form became an early proving ground for the playwright who would later collapse the past into the present to stage the life of an entire village, and who would include the Ice Age, the Deluge, and a world war in a single three-act play.

The majority of these three-minute plays explore competing visions of time through one simple technique: they divorce well-known characters from their usual environments and force them to function in different times or in unfamiliar contexts. In one play Mozart, worrying over his poverty and despairing of a commission, is interrupted in his practical considerations by a commission from Death. Here, the concerns of the earthly world and human time contrast with those of the spiritual world and eternity, implying their concurrent but conflicting demands for our attention. Another play presents the death of Childe Roland, whose dying prayer to the Blessed Virgin is answered not by the Queen of Heaven he addresses, but by three mystical queens in a mythic dark tower, entrance to the underworld of a time period and a system of beliefs different from those he invokes.

In another play from this collection, entitled *Proserpina and the Devil*, Wilder's instinct for compression takes on an added dimension as he first conflates the traditions of classical mythology with those of Christianity and then inserts them into a seventeenth-century Venetian marionette show. On this puppet stage, the Lake of Wrath serves as the River Styx, Noah's Ark as Charon's barge, Pluto as Satan, Hermes as the Archangel Gabriel, and "a handsome Italian matron" (29) in stiff brocade as Demeter. Wilder's interest in the repeated cycles of time is apparent here in this interchanging of mythic and religious figures in the more recent—although still historical—context of seventeenth-century Italy. His abridgement of time also demonstrates the ways in which the details of a workaday routine—represented in the play by the difficulties of the puppeteers, or the "matter of pins and hooks-and-eyes" (29) that prevents Proserpina's rescue—can obscure the interaction of larger contexts, which shape and are shaped by the event itself.

In one three-minute play, *Fanny Otcott*, Wilder explores with some success both his interest in competing perspectives and his concern for the interaction between historical patterns and particular moments. *Fanny Otcott* is structurally different from its companion pieces in two important ways. Unlike many of the other plays, which present only the static meditations of ready-made mythic or historic figures, *Fanny Otcott* contains an evolving plot. The climax occurs when Fanny recognizes the possibilities afforded by conflicting interpretations of events past and present. In addition, in *Fanny Otcott* Wilder focuses his inquiries on one character's view of her personal past and so emphasizes both individual perception and the particular moment with an immediacy unmatched in the volume.

Against the backdrop of an Arthurian tower—a reminder that Fanny's situation has often been repeated through history—the aging actress Fanny Otcott sorts out her souvenirs—"in short, her past" (33). Enter George, her long-ago lover and now a bishop, whose memories of his former "association" (33) with Fanny are very different from her own. What Fanny remembers with tenderness and delight—"It was like hawthorn-buds and meadow larks and Mr. Handel's Water-music" (36)—George recalls as "a distressing spot on my conscience" (37). The play ends as Fanny dismisses the illusory memory world she has so long inhabited and resolves to rejoice in present life rather than in recollections of the past.

This is the earliest clear-cut instance in Wilder's dramatic canon of a dilemma his later plays insist upon: Fanny cannot seize the day if she insists on burying it with memories, but neither can she recognize the ultimate importance of the present moment if she isolates it from its place in the developing patterns of her life. The validity of the concept by which she has lived—that is, her interpretation of her affair with George—is called into question by George's conflicting recollections, and the possibility that contradictory patterns can emerge from a single event becomes clear to her. Fanny now recognizes that her own perception of a single past episode has shaped her entire past, present, and future. Although this recognition affirms the intrinsic significance of both that defining moment and her unique perception of it, it simultaneously suggests that the importance of a particular moment is undiscoverable until that moment has been absorbed into a larger context. By the end of this short play Fanny achieves a new awareness, as she seizes the present moment of the play—her disappointing reunion with George—to alter both her understanding of the past and the development of her future. She learns that living in the past obscures the value of the present.

Fanny's final recognition that an individual's interpretation of the past is the past that matters most seems to parallel a growing awareness of Wilder's. Throughout his next ten years of technical exploration with the one-act form, Wilder would continue to examine the invasion of the present by past decisions and the distance in time needed to see the effects of such decisions—the central dilemma that would inform all his formal experiments and culminate in the achievement of *Our Town*.

The Rediscovery of Forgotten Goods

The young Wilder's precocious creativity in presenting stage time as both flexible and variable is evident in his three-minute plays, but their obviously contrived form produced insoluble problems as well. The interesting devices Wilder was learning to employ in these plays most often have lyric rather than dramatic effects, and the brief moments of the plays usually remain static, lacking climax or direction. By abolishing time, these plays demonstrate the young Wilder's tendency to "experiment with form before he had troubled to think up an adequate plot."[6]

Wilder's youthful digressions from traditional dramatic form are easy to understand, however, in the light of the overly plotted, inflexible dramatic models available to an aspiring young playwright in 1920s America. As described in the first chapter, the American stage at that time (with a few notable exceptions) was deeply entrenched in a formal realism much too rigid to have supported the overlapping temporal perspectives that interested Wilder. Like Eugene O'Neill, Wilder lamented the reductive vision of time demanded by the proscenium stage. In Wilder's view, the playwrights and producers of the conventionally realistic theatre had "shut the play up into a museum showcase"; they had "loaded the stage with specific objects," each of which

> fixes and narrows the action to one moment in time and place. . . . When you emphasize *place* in the theatre, you drag down and limit and harness time to it. You thrust the action back into the past time, whereas it is precisely the glory of the stage that it is always "now" there.[7]

By rejecting its pretenses, the drama had forfeited its ability to telescope time, remaining content to mirror events significant only at a certain moment. On the proscenium stage, where time was "harnessed" to place, the past could no longer collide with the present in diverse and unexpected ways.

The problems confronting the young Wilder were thus manifold: formal realism had atrophied contemporary dramatic form, and his own three-minute plays were structurally weak, in one sense even evading the issue of stage time. How, then, was he to develop a form suitable for embodying conflicting visions of time? In his classical education Wilder found a partial answer to this question; he discovered that

> the history of the theatre shows us that in its greatest ages the stage employed the greatest number of conventions. The stage is fundamental pretense and it thrives on the acceptance of that fact and in the multiplication of additional pretenses.[8]

If few twentieth-century American playwrights had been able to develop new conventions for expressing contemporary attitudes toward time's passing, at least some of the drama's old vitality could be restored by rejuvenating its old conventions. Wilder therefore turned to the drama of past centuries and foreign countries. If the dramatic models available to him were incompatible with his design, then he would find alternative models.

As William A. Scally has noted, Wilder borrowed techniques for presenting "cyclic history" from the British medieval mystery plays.[9] Other eras and other places provided other models. In the works of the Elizabethans, Wilder discovered the freedom that antimimetic staging could produce; as he says of *Romeo and Juliet:*

> When the play is staged as Shakespeare intended it, the bareness of the

stage releases the events from the particular and the experience of Juliet partakes of that of all girls in love, in every time, place, and language.[10]

In the works of the Japanese Noh dramatists, in which an actor's circling the stage represents a long journey and the passage of much time, Wilder discovered a similar freedom. And like O'Neill, who had recognized in the works of the new German expressionist playwrights a method for depicting a subjective reality, Wilder found in the expressionists and particularly in Bertolt Brecht some contemporary methods for breaking down the outdated verisimilitude, with its linear relationship between past and present, of the proscenium stage.

Wilder's theatrical debt to Brecht has attracted much critical attention.[11] Wilder's thematic interests are very different from Brecht's— "humanistic" rather than "Marxist," to borrow a pair of convenient, albeit reductive, labels—but his methods of staging and his exuberant theatricality partake heavily of Brecht's own. Like Brecht, who exaggerates theatrical gestures and emphasizes conventions to produce his notorious "alienation effect," Wilder frequently uses an intrusive Stage Manager, self-conscious characters, and a disregard for chronological time; like Brecht, Wilder insists on the reality of theatre as theatre. For Wilder, however, the separate reality of theatre does not necessarily impose distance between audience and character; rather, it establishes the equal validity of multiple temporal contexts. By combining Brechtian theatricality, Elizabethan flexibility of space, and expressionistic distortions of time and perspective, Wilder synthesized a form that permitted him to portray concurrent yet rival perspectives on the passage of time.

Despite his enormous creativity in adapting techniques and developing a plastic dramatic form, Wilder himself minimized his own importance in rejuvenating the American theatre. As he expressed it, his experiments with dramatic form were mere stepping-stones for more talented playwrights:

> The theatre has lagged behind the other arts in finding the "new ways" to express how men and women feel in our time. I am not one of the new dramatists we are looking for. I wish I were. I hope I have played a part in preparing the way for them. I am not an innovator but a rediscoverer of forgotten goods and a remover of obtrusive bric-a-brac.[12]

Here, Wilder seems to have underestimated the importance of his particular moment (or imagination) in both absorbing and shaping general historical patterns—in this case, the inherited pattern of dramatic form. He was, in fact, a consummate innovator, the novelty of his mature work apparent in his new uses and original syntheses of restored techniques.

Before Wilder could effectively "unharness" stage time in full-length plays, however, he experimented with rival visions of time in one-act plays. These plays demonstrate the variety of techniques he had recovered to depict both the impact of time's passage and the many ways of viewing it.

Somewhere Where Time Passes

Wilder returned from his 1928 lecture tour of Europe armed with an entire new arsenal of antimimetic techniques, prepared to attack the reductive vision of the realistic stage. He proposed to bombard that "abject realism" which he saw as "deeply in earnest, every detail is true, but the whole finally tumbles to the ground—true but without significance."[13] The variety of the experiments in *The Long Christmas Dinner and Other Plays in One Act* attests to the vigor of his attack.

The title play of the volume dramatizes the interaction between passing moments and repeated patterns; it also demonstrates Wilder's maturing techniques for depicting rather than merely repudiating stage time. *The Long Christmas Dinner* presents a single occasion—the Bayard family's annual Christmas dinner—that evolves into a larger pattern of inherited traditions as it is repeated yearly. The ninety years of annual Christmas dinners pass in a continuum, unbroken by act divisions, scenery changes, or other abrupt transitions of the formally realistic stage. Characters simply enter the dining room when they are born or marry into the family and exit when they move away or die. In effect, the ninety-year cycle of repeated ritual becomes, on the stage, only one event, with one setting, one action—in short, one long, unbroken Christmas dinner despite the gradual alterations in its component parts. In this way, the present includes the past, each dinner is all dinners, and the particular moment expands to encompass the entire historical pattern.

As time passes and the play progresses, however, the participants at the dinner change: the baby carriage that stands near the table is eventually replaced by an adult actor, who later expresses the passage of even more time by donning a gray wig. As each character matures, he or she inherits a new role within the family hierarchy and reshapes that role according to his or her individual responses to it. The passage of time is thus linked to the inevitability of change: although the reenactment of certain familial roles by successive characters implies continuity of the pattern, the joys and griefs of each character are immediate, unprecedented, and contribute in unique ways to the development of that pattern.

Within this cycle of evolution and repetition, some things change and some endure. The circular structure of the play emphasizes repetition: *The Long Christmas Dinner* begins and ends with the reflections of an elderly woman—in each case called "Mother Bayard" by the members of her family—on enjoying her first Christmas dinner in her grown child's new home. Each woman's outlook on her Christmas dinner party is unique, however, and these differences in detail affirm each character's role in shaping the inherited rituals. The rituals themselves endure, but they change by retaining the imprint of each character who has enacted them.

In other instances this change is emphasized, as the patterns and beliefs of one generation are modified by the next. Charles' assertion that "time certainly goes by very fast in a great new country like this" is refuted by his impatient son Roderick, who claims: "Time passes so slowly here that it stands still, that's what's the trouble. . . . I'm going somewhere where time passes."[14] Here, Roderick shares his father's confusion of time with place but disagrees about the rate at which it passes. And in a number of instances throughout the play, a single, familial role—mother, sister, cousin—is filled successively by characters from different generations and demonstrates explicitly the mutually shaping effects of repeated patterns and individual responses, of past history and present moments.

In *The Long Christmas Dinner* Wilder successfully dramatized the past as a shifting yet essential part of the present; the characters may modify the patterns they have inherited, but the patterns continue to direct their actions. The wonder felt by each character at a repeated, special event—the birth of a baby, a twig wrapped in ice ("You almost never see that," we are told on four separate occasions—3, 10, 13, 25)—illustrates Wilder's vision of an event as both an individual experience and a part of a larger context, apparent only through time. And because the form of the play depicts the restructuring through time of a single, repeated event, the passage of time becomes a felt experience as well as a central theme. The play beautifully illustrates both the concern for the past Wilder shared with his compatriots and the differences from them engendered by his interest in competing temporal contexts.

Other plays in this volume explore the effects of time in quite different ways and demonstrate the real flexibility that Wilder was now bringing to the stage. While in *The Long Christmas Dinner* Wilder compressed nearly a century of Bayard family history into one half-hour of stage time and so provided a sweeping retrospective viewpoint, in *Pullman Car Hiawatha* he employed an opposite strategy. The play presents a total cross-section, from personal detail to cosmic context, of a single moment in time—the moment of Harriet's death. By halting time to focus on one event, Wilder is able to dramatize concurrent but conflicting temporal contexts.

The most obvious context is human time—the time of Harriet's life, which is now at an end. What life has meant to Harriet becomes clear in her farewell speech:

> Goodbye, 1312 Ridgewood Avenue, Oaksbury, Illinois. I hope I remember all its steps and doors and wallpapers forever. Goodbye, Emerson Grammar School on the corner of Forbush Avenue and Wherry Street. Goodbye, Miss Walker and Miss Cramer who taught me English and Miss Matthewson who taught me Biology. Goodbye, First Congregational Church on the corner of Meyerson Avenue and Sixth Street and Dr. McReady and Mrs. McReady and Julia. Goodbye, Papa and Mama. (68)

Seen from this unique, retrospective viewpoint, time passes imperceptibly in an accumulation of details with significance only for the person involved. And while Harriet's farewell speech is clearly meant to move us, Wilder nevertheless takes pains in this play to show that the perspective of memory is limited, and that other time frames impart different sorts of meaning.

This becomes apparent through the actions of the Stage Manager. At the moment of Harriet's death, the Stage Manager breaks into the action and abruptly enlarges the prevailing viewpoint:

> All right. So much for the inside of the car. That'll be enough of that for the present. Now for its position geographically, astronomically, theologically considered.
> Pullman Car Hiawatha, ten minutes of ten. December twenty-first, 1930. All ready. (58)

This sudden shift from the living and dying inside the train to conditions exterior to it forces us to acknowledge alternative ways of viewing the action. The moving train passes through a variety of contexts as it travels through an ever-changing landscape and through numerous systems for measuring time. By shifting the focus away from Harriet, the Stage Manager forces us to accept the limits of a human perspective on time.

Despite the convergence of these general contexts at the moment of Harriet's death, however, life on the Pullman Car Hiawatha is given an emphasis equal, within the framework of this play, to that given the local geography, the weather, and the stars; Harriet's death is in no way trivialized. In fact, none of the larger systems for measuring time—astronomical, geological, meteorological, theological—imparted nearly so much meaning to Harriet's life as did the domestic details she remembers. The Stage Manager's final action underscores the importance of particular human vision in both generating and acknowledging systems for measuring time. Although his role as central intelligence has permitted him to view all time frames equally as they converge, in his final action he chooses a limited and local perspective from which to view events. He abandons his managerial role and closes out the play as the particularly clumsy passenger in Upper Berth Five.

Despite his implication in *Pullman Car Hiawatha* that the individual or the local point of view provides the best vantage point from which to assess the importance of events, in *The Happy Journey from Trenton to Camden* the playwright explores the perils of maintaining too limited a perspective. In technique, this play is similar to its companion pieces: as in *The Long Christmas Dinner,* time is compressed, and a three-hour car trip takes only about fifteen minutes of stage time; as in *Pullman Car Hiawatha,* the characters ride an imaginary vehicle moving through time and space, represented on the stage only by a few suggestive boards and four chairs. This play differs from the others, however, in that it offers no temporal perspective between the uniquely personal and the eternal. Lacking intermediary contexts—such as the repeated family roles of the Bayards or the "geographical, meteorological, and astronomical" considerations through which the Pullman Car Hiawatha passes on its way to eternity—the daily routines of the Kirbys seem petty and inconsequential.

Early in their journey, the Kirbys must stop to allow a funeral procession to pass, and when they reach their destination we learn that the convalescent daughter they have traveled to visit has lost a newborn child. The twin deaths in the play are thus set in relief against the details of Kirby family life, and their response to the deaths illustrates their single-mindedness: despite the mysteries of death and afterlife, life must continue, the chicken must be roasted for dinner, and the loss of Beulah's child must not interfere with the functioning of the family unit. As Ma Kirby tells her daughter, "God thought best. We don't understand why. We just go on, honey, doin' our business" (121). Unlike *The Long Christmas Dinner*, which spans nearly a century, or *Pullman Car Hiawatha*, which includes representatives of the entire galaxy, the world presented in *The Happy Journey* is totally grounded in the present. By the end of the play Ma Kirby's habitual recitation of proverbial wisdom becomes a rather annoying drone, and the colossal backdrop of eternity against which the Kirbys continue their homely activities serves only to diminish their importance.

The Happy Journey thus presents a vision of the world that is almost as narrow as that of the realistic stage Wilder eschewed. Yet the unconventional staging—reminiscent of the Elizabethan methods that Wilder admired—does offer us a new way of observing the limitations of such an artificially confined perspective.

In recovering forgotten conventions to compose the plays in this volume, Wilder developed an impressive array of antimimetic techniques. When transferred to his full-length plays, these techniques allowed Wilder to portray time as something that moves in diverse ways and the past as something always encapsulated in the present, despite the limited and varying vantage points from which it can be viewed.

The Life of the Village and the Life of the Stars

In an early preface to *Our Town* (written with the play in 1938, but not published until 1979), Wilder uses an intriguing metaphor to explain the play's multiple ways of viewing time. He had tried to present, as he said, "the life of the village against the life of the stars."[15] *Our Town* does present "the life of the village," with its cyclic, daily patterns and its locally shared assumptions, enacted in loving detail by the inhabitants of Grover's Corners. The larger eternal patterns represented by "the life of the stars" also play a significant part in the action, as questions about birth, death, and afterlife occasionally interrupt the diurnality of the action, especially when introduced directly to the audience by the Stage Manager. As a result of these conflicting yet concurrent methods of portraying life on the stage, the audience is continually forced to select, from among several points in time, a place to stand and view the action.

The necessity of such a choice is dramatized in act 3, when Emily returns posthumously to Grover's Corners to relive her twelfth birthday. At this point Emily, now dead, is largely the product of all she has been; her parents, her girlhood relationship with George, her life as a farm wife have all combined to color her perceptions and form her identity. She cannot, therefore, be again what she once was, and her now mature reliving of her twelfth birthday demonstrates explicitly—both to her and to the audience—the impossibility of recovering the past or of unraveling the patterns of life once they have been woven. The value of a seemingly trivial moment (in this case, Emily's birthday) is thus seen from the twofold perspective of past and present: the first demonstrates the moment's importance in developing the pattern of a lifetime; the second proclaims its intrinsic worth as something fleeting and unrepeatable.

This twofold interpretation of a present moment is offered throughout the play by the Stage Manager, who operates within two worlds—that of the production and that of the play—at once. His very first speech demonstrates his ability to function in both contexts, as he introduces the cast of players and the inhabitants of Grover's Corners almost simultaneously. In his role as a theatrical device, the Stage Manager single-handedly runs the show: he acts as a living playbill, he describes and prepares the imaginary set, he directs the actors, and he often interrupts the play to comment on the future significance of an action just presented. By intruding in this way between the audience and the characters, he permits us to share his double vision of present and future (which Emily achieves only after her death in the third act) from the very beginning of the play.

Early in the play the Stage Manager offers us our first choice of time frames, and the response we must inevitably make directs our attention to the importance of the present moment. The Stage Manager allows us to eavesdrop on a conversation between the town's current paper boy, Joe Crowell, and Dr. Gibbs, as both go about their early morning routines:

Dr. Gibbs. Anything serious goin' on in the world since Wednesday?
Joe Crowell, Jr. Yessir. My schoolteacher, Miss Foster, 's getting married to a fella over in Concord.[16]

This brief interchange between neighbors establishes the importance of community events and also indicates the limited perspective of a Grover's Corners youth, to whom the marriage of a teacher has national significance. The Stage Manager, however, in an attempt to broaden the temporal viewpoint, stops the action to reveal Joe's future:

Want to tell you something about that boy Joe Crowell there. Joe was awful bright—graduated from high school here, head of his class. So he got a scholarship to Massachusetts Tech. Graduated head of his class there, too. It was all wrote up in the Boston paper at the time. Goin' to be a great engineer, Joe was. But the war broke out and he died in France.—All that education for nothing. (9)

The Stage Manager clearly has the ability to foretell the future, but his balanced viewpoint offers only a part of the picture. Within the pattern of world war, Joe's education was, certainly, meaningless, but within the pattern of life in Grover's Corners, Joe's academic accomplishment stands out as a significant achievement in his short life and a model of success in his community. The Stage Manager's timeless perspective would rob Joe of his achievements, but attention to the actual moment of Joe's success would preserve them. Evidently much of the dignity and value of daily life depends on a limited temporal perspective, one that disregards the formation of larger patterns and focuses on the present moment.

The Stage Manager's awareness of the future does not always blind him to the benefits of attending to the present, however; in fact, he often shrinks his own extended frame of reference by presenting the immediate impact of a moment along with its historical significance. That he does value immediacy is clearly evident when he presents the drug store scene, in which George and Emily first recognize their love for one another. The Stage Manager introduces the event by interrupting George and Emily's wedding and placing the drug store scene within the general context of "Love and Marriage" (the title of the second act):

Now I have to interrupt again here. You see, we want to know how all this began—this wedding, this plan to spend a lifetime together. I'm awfully interested in how big things like that begin. You know how it is: you're twenty-one or twenty-two and you make some decisions; then whissh! you're seventy: you've been a lawyer for fifty years, and that white-haired lady at your side has eaten over fifty thousand meals with you. How do such things begin? (60)

After establishing the drug store incident as a "big thing" in forming the pattern of George and Emily's future, however, the Stage Manager reminds us in an unabashed appeal to our emotions of some of the special properties intrinsic to the moment itself, qualities that are immediate and understandable only from a short-term perspective:

George and Emily are going to show you now the conversation that they had when they first knew that . . . that . . . as the saying goes . . . they were meant for each other. But before they do I want you to remember what it was like to have been very young. And particularly the days when you were first in love: when you were like a person sleepwalking, and you didn't quite see the street you were in, and didn't quite hear everything that was said to you. You're just a little bit crazy. Will you remember that, please? (60)

The Stage Manager's direct commentary on the number of ways one can view this scene is not his most important contribution to it, however; he also emphasizes the moment by shifting it from its ordinary dramatic context. In a formally realistic play, this meeting between George and Emily would have been a focal point in time, a traditional, second-act "recognition scene." By interrupting the present day of the action (that is, George and Emily's wedding day) to introduce the recognition scene in a flashback, out of temporal sequence, he stresses the magic of the moment itself, outside any larger pattern, isolated in time. Furthermore, by modifying standard three-act form and presenting incidents nonsequentially, he repeats a familiar pattern (here, traditional dramatic form) by altering one of its components (the formally realistic handling of stage time). In this way he recapitulates in a theatrical context the constant reevaluating of particular moments in terms of developing patterns that the characters enact in the alternative world of Grover's Corners.

But even this theatrical exemplification of the play's thematic patterns is not always specific enough to ensure our attention to the moment at hand. It demands the Stage Manager's continued presence in a world outside that of the action and so implies that present action cannot display its own worth. To counteract this suggestion and so emphasize even more completely the value of the moment in a world of multiple temporal frameworks, the Stage Manager occasionally renounces his ability to foresee the future and becomes, at least temporarily, an ordinary citizen of Grover's Corners. In the recognition scene he jumps from his role as Stage Manager to become, with the addition of a pair of spectacles, the proprietor of Morgan's drug store. George and Emily's discussion there is important not only for the pattern of future events and family and community relationships it initiates (and which the Stage Manager describes), but also for the excitement and emotional impact of the moment itself (which Mr. Morgan shares and cheerfully approves). By alternating his all-knowing theatrical role with that of a specific character, the Stage Manager is able to study historical patterns and also to participate in momentary events. In this way he embodies the tensions that continually inform *Our Town*.

The importance of a particular moment is demonstrated so compellingly in this recognition in part because of the groundwork laid for it in act 1. The real "action" of act 1 is extremely limited: we are shown a community of simple characters performing their daily, habitual tasks. The act builds up no conflict, no potential clash between antagonists. In fact, if act 1 has any relationship to traditional dramatic form it is in the repetition of details and the circularity of daily activities that, by suggesting perpetual reenactment, expose the past while depicting the present. The act moves placidly through the events of a typical Grover's Corners day: predawn newspaper deliveries and the children's breakfast give way to stringing beans and baseball practice, which in turn make way for the evening meal and the smell of heliotrope in a moonlit garden. The circularity of these events is underscored by direct references to the life cycle, including the babies born in the first few minutes of the act and the impending death of Simon Stimson (choir master and genteel town drunk) at the end.

This finely focused attention to repeated detail and specific moments characterizes both the first and second acts of *Our Town*. Act 3, however, reverses the emphasis of the first two acts, as the death of Emily forces us to notice the larger perspectives of life and death, with only occasional references to the routines of "Daily Life" or the inherited patterns of "Love and Marriage." Just as the value of the moment was challenged in the first two acts by intermittent references to the necessity of a historical perspective, so in this act the larger temporal perspective is challenged by the local, immediate point of view that preceded it. This contrast is emphasized in the Stage Manager's opening soliloquy, in which he says:

> Now, there are some things we all know, but we don't take'm out and look at'm very often. We all know that *something* is eternal, and that something has to do with human beings. All the greatest people ever lived have been telling us that for five thousand years and yet you'd be surprised how people are always losing hold of it. There's something way down deep that's eternal about every human being. (81)

In this way, the Stage Manager directs our attention away from the individual moments of life to the eternal importance of every individual. This time, however, he includes the audience specifically in his analysis. In describing the changes in Grover's Corners since act 2, he points not to stage left or stage right (as he did in act 1), but directly into the audience to locate the scene of the action. From the mountaintop cemetery on which he now stands—implying the more distanced, perhaps more elevated perspective he commands—the members of the audience become the living citizens of Grover's Corners. Because of our previous attention to (and eventual inclusion in) the daily moments of Grover's Corners, we are now offered a richer and more immediate understanding of the universal and the timeless.

In accordance with this reversal of emphasis in act 3, the structure of the act is also somewhat different from that of the first two. The present action of act 3 is interrupted by an important scene presented out of sequence, out of its usual place in the context of chronological time, as was that of act 2; the return to Emily's twelfth birthday in act 3, however, is more than a mere flashback, since this time Emily shares our retrospective view. Instead of merely acting out a scene for us, conscious only of the present, in act 3 Emily is painfully aware of the future significance of the events she relives. The resultant dramatic irony allows her to acknowledge the value of each fleeting moment and to lament her current inability to recapture it. Her double perspective on her own life forces her tormented question, "Do human beings ever realize life while they live it?—every, every minute?" (100).

The routines of daily life that began acts 1 and 2 are thus relegated to this past scene in act 3, since the routines of daily life are now merely a cherished memory for Emily, framed within the boundaries of eternity. As she enters the kitchen for breakfast on her birthday morning, Emily is immediately bombarded with details she had either forgotten or never even noticed. Her new awareness of her past obliviousness causes her great pain. "I can't look at everything hard enough," she cries (97) as she observes that her mother had once been young and remembers a long-forgotten childhood gift from George. Her new double perspective permits her to see not only that each moment of life is priceless, but also, as Simon Stimson tells her, that to be alive is to "move about in a cloud of ignorance; to go up and down trampling the feelings of those . . . of those about you. To spend and waste time as though you had a million years" (101).

The value of memory thus seems both a blessing and a curse: it enables Emily finally to appreciate the defining details of her own ended life, but it also illuminates the human inability to recognize the important moments of life until they have passed.[17] Emily's double perspective allows her to see the multiple time frames at work during her life, and to recognize that the most limited of these is the one for which she will grieve most. In an echo of Harriet's farewell to life in *Pullman Car Hiawatha*, Emily addresses time and enumerates the details that she now sees as having been most significant in defining her identity on earth:

> Good-by, Good-by, world. Good-by, Grover's Corners . . . Mama and Papa. Good-by to clocks ticking . . . and Mama's sunflowers. And food and coffee. And new-ironed dresses and hot baths . . . and sleeping and waking up. Oh, earth, you're too wonderful for anybody to realize you. (100)

The ultimate value of a timeless perspective, it seems, is the insight it can afford into the value of the particular moment. Emily's return to the graveyard places the final emphasis on the importance of specific events and unrepeatable moments in a world crowded with competing temporal contexts, as she resumes her place within that peaceful void, the solitary context of eternity. There, the details of life gradually fade from the memories of the graveyard inhabitants (like Mrs. Gibbs, who can no longer remember the names of the stars), and the characters, cut off from the concerns and routines of daily living, drift away from life itself. As the Stage Manager tells us:

> You know as well as I do that the dead don't stay interested in us living people for very long. Gradually, gradually, they lose hold of the earth . . .

and the ambitions they had . . . and the things they suffered . . . and the people they loved. They get weaned away from the earth. . . . (81)

Life in *Our Town*, finally, consists of a multitude of interacting systems for evaluating time, from those of the village to those of the stars. The ones that most clearly define and enrich life, however, are those that distract, disorder, and confuse the inhabitants and so protect them from death's timeless void: the ones composed of each character's ambitions and sufferings and joys, of significant details, of a limited perspective, and of cherished, particular events. The unusual structure of the play successfully embodies Wilder's ambition to "represent the Act in Eternity"[18]—that is, to depict the importance of each fleeting moment within the ever-expanding boundaries of time.

Circumstances Variously Reported

In *Our Town*, Wilder employed firsthand what he saw in the Elizabethans: that a simply staged play could universalize the particular without denying the impact of individual moments. But Wilder was also interested, as his early plays show, in the changes that time brings, in the patterns that time creates from seemingly isolated present moments. In *The Skin of Our Teeth* Wilder used an overt theatricalism akin to Brecht's to demonstrate the importance of passing moments in unfolding history, regardless of the limited perspective of an individual acting at a given time.

From the opening of *The Skin of Our Teeth*, the audience is bombarded with an array of conflicting details; we cannot locate the characters in a specific time or place because both keep changing. The curtain does not even rise as the play begins but rather becomes a projection screen for slides of the daily "News Events of the World." In this curious newscast, the scrubwomen who clean the theatre are pictured and introduced, allowing the world of the theatre and the production to intrude into the world of the performance before the action can even begin. Another news item advertises a wedding ring currently in the theatre's lost and found, inscribed "To Eva from Adam. Genesis II:18," and so invokes a wider set of contexts—historical, temporal, biblical. The ring will be returned to its owner only with proper identification, however, and so the world of legal documents and credentials encroaches upon the context of theatre, the contexts of love and marriage, and the contexts of time and religion. The limitations of all these perspectives are made clear by the next slide: a wall of ice that "has not yet been satisfactorily explained" is disrupting communication and pushing a cathedral— monument of human aspirations—from Montreal to Vermont.[19]

Contexts continue to overlap at this unprecedented rate throughout the play. In this way, Wilder once again poses the question that Emily had asked in *Our Town:* how is it possible to assess the value of the present until it has become part of the past, part of a pattern recognizable only through time? In *The Skin of Our Teeth*, once again, Wilder suggests the near impossibility of doing so.

Wilder draws attention to this concern primarily by collapsing temporal distinctions: the Ice Age in act 1 turns into both the antediluvian world and the New Jersey boardwalk in act 2, only to become a twentieth-century postwar city in act 3. Within this multitemporal framework, repeated patterns are emphasized because everybody assumes multiple identities. Henry Antrobus is four thousand years old, but a little boy; Sabina is a scullery maid, boardwalk beauty queen, camp follower, and Sabine woman, all at the same time. George Antrobus has recently "discovered" the wheel, a detail that defines George as a prehistoric man, an inventor, an explorer, or perhaps all three; he lives in the suburbs (conveniently located near a church, a school, and an A & P), a context that locates him in modern New Jersey; he has been a gardener (Adam?) but left the position "under circumstances which have been variously reported" (111); and he is a veteran of foreign wars, symbol of the omnipresent human conflict inevitably produced by competing contexts. Like the Bayards in *The Long Christmas Dinner,* who enact repeated but changing familial roles, the Antrobus family of *The Skin of Our Teeth* demonstrate the continuity of all human experience, throughout all time.

Within this palimpsest of competing chronologies and perspectives, every action of the characters is in some undetermined way important and in some way influences the course of events or the evolution of human beings. No present action can be seen as trivial in a world where George's decision to put the family pets out overnight leads to the extinction of the mammoth and the dinosaur, and where the audience's passing their chairs up to the stage can help "save the human race" (159). From the beginning of the play, then, we are faced, as are the characters, with a universe of overlapping time frames, in which any event or any decision can have undreamed-of repercussions, and in which the significance of each moment becomes clear only when that moment has been engulfed by the past.

A play enacting multiple eras and embodying competing temporal viewpoints is not, of course, reducible to any simple thematic coherence; no one interpretation of an event or a moment ever seems sufficient in *The Skin of Our Teeth*. This becomes abundantly clear during the rehearsal scene, when Mr. Fitzpatrick, the stage manager, interrupts the play to rehearse some last-minute understudies (supposedly the cleaning crew of the theatre) because several of the actors have become ill. This rehearsal scene obviously underscores the importance of time in the play, since the passing hours of evening are depicted as characters quoting philosophers' thoughts. While explaining the scene to the audience, Mr. Fitzpatrick mentions that the personification of time doesn't "mean anything. It's just a kind of poetic effect" (216). The actress Miss Somerset, however, vehemently disagrees: "Not mean anything! Why, it certainly does. . . . I think it means that when people are asleep they have all those lovely thoughts, much better than when they're awake" (216). And Ivy, Miss Somerset's maid, presents yet another analysis of the playwright's device:

> The author meant that—just like the hours and stars go over our heads at night, in the same way the ideas and thoughts of the great men are in the air around us all the time and they're working on us, even when we don't know it. (217)

The irony of all these conflicts of interpretation is apparent in the passage from Spinoza (otherwise known as "Nine o'clock"), which asserts that "all the objects of my desire and fear were in themselves nothing good nor bad save insofar as the mind was affected by them" (219). In short, the subject of the scene is that the meanings of things can be determined only from an individual point of view and in the fullness of time; the action of the scene and the disagreement between the characters serve principally to dramatize the alternative perspectives that passing time demands.

Competing time frames and perspectives are thus much more than virtuoso technical devices in *The Skin of Our Teeth;* they are an actual subject of the play. *The Skin of Our Teeth* offers us, finally, a glimpse at the unlimited (if sometimes unrecognized) possibilities inherent in a

world of rival contexts. What makes those possibilities recognizable in
the pluralistic world of the play is Wilder's telescoping of stage time:
by providing retrospective and future viewpoints simultaneously with
an immediate one, Wilder demonstrates the value of the moment in
creating history.

The Act in Eternity

In Thornton Wilder's two major full-length plays as well as in a
number of his shorter ones, he stressed the importance of each
present moment, each choice, in determining as yet unrecognizable
historical patterns. Whether his technique for expressing such a
theme included the intermingling of historical eras, the
achronological rendering of stage time, or the presentation of events
on an unlocalized, unbounded stage, it always typified his "effort to
find the dignity in the trivial of our daily life, against those pre-
posterous stretches which seem to rob it of any dignity."[20] One is
always aware, when watching a Wilder play, that present moments
play a starring role in determining what will become the past.

What I hope is clear by now is that Wilder's contributions to
American drama are not so different from those of his more frequently
studied compatriots. He shares their awareness of the past's multiple
relationships with the present, and he shares their interest in developing conventions to explore those relationships. Like O'Neill, Wilder
began his career by exploding the proscenium stage and ended by
exploiting that explosion, inviting the audience to share the experiences of his characters. Like Miller, he asserts that each moment,
each choice, is part of a larger pattern; the difference here is that
Miller focuses on the specific pattern of causation, while Wilder
refuses to limit his perspectives at all. And like Williams, Wilder
experiments with dramatic conventions to portray "two times at
once," even though Williams's interest in the double vision of remembered time and chronological time is narrower in scope than Wilder's
collapsing of eras.

In the light of Wilder's constant attempts to reconcile the particular
moment with the larger forces of history, it seems fitting that his own
place in the American drama should be assessed not only by the
specific events that are the plays themselves, but also by their place in
creating modern dramatic form. In part because of Wilder's "rediscov-

ery of forgotten goods" and his combination of diverse elements into a flexible vehicle for expressing contemporary concerns, the American drama has moved away from the confines of formal realism to become an arena of evolving possibilities. In short, the "disparate moment" that is Thornton Wilder's dramatic canon has forever altered the "repetitive pattern" of inherited dramatic form.

4

Arthur Miller

Illuminating Process

According to Arthur Miller, modern drama too often depicts a world devoid of causal logic, where language loses its conventional meaning, the familiar is removed from its usual context, and actions produce few predictable results. Miller's quintessential theme, in contrast, is that people are responsible for what they create, that "consequences of actions are as real as the actions themselves."[1] In order to express this equal "reality" of actions and consequences, causes and effects, it becomes imperative to establish what the past entails and how it affects the present. In Arthur Miller's stage world, therefore, even more than in those of his American contemporaries, the past is always a crucial defining element of the present.

Miller describes his own playwriting career as a series of attempts to portray this equal reality of actions and consequences. He says:

> I've always done the same thing in one way or another—and that is to show the process. It's the way my mind works—to ask how something came to be what it is, rather than to play upon the apparent surfaces of things to give a sense of what they are.[2]

This concept of a direct connection between past and present, between "how something came to be" and what it now is, would seem to be the very concept of the past best suited to the well-made play and the proscenium stage. In fact, Miller's early plays do follow the formulas of stage realism rather closely. But when Miller uses the term "process" for relating past and present, he is moving toward a very different notion of their relationship from that exemplified in the formal stage realism, with its given past and predictable consequences, of his early career. What changes from play to play in Miller's canon is his notion of this relationship betwen past and present, and thus of the "process" by which the causal past is partly discovered and partly constituted in being persistently explored.

Early in his career Miller turned to Ibsen and his retrospective method to document the lingering effects of the past on the present. He followed the Norwegian's lead in beginning his own formally realistic plays close to the crisis of the story, then gradually revealing the forces that precipitated the crisis. "I connected with Ibsen," Miller has said, ". . . because he was illuminating process":

> [Ibsen's view] is profoundly dynamic, for that enormous past was always heavily documented to the end that the present be comprehended with wholeness, as a moment in a flow of time, and not—as with so many modern plays—as a situation without roots.[3]

As discussed in the first chapter, however, the past that informs Ibsenian realistic plays is usually an indisputable, externally verifiable chain of events, a linear causal sequence which the characters recognize as such. The "process" illuminated in such plays is thus limited to an uncovering of past secrets—the missing links in the chain—as the temporal sequence of the plot determines the extent of a character's responsibility for his or her actions.

As Miller matured as a dramatist, however, he began to transfer his own dramatic problem of determing causality onto his characters. The causal relationships that in an Ibsenian thesis play are known to the characters and must be revealed to the audience become, in Miller's mature plays, something the characters themselves must investigate and determine individually. The "process" that Miller illuminates thus develops from an uncovering of external plot sequence to an internal voyage of discovery.

When such psychological process assumes dramatic priority, causes and effects are no longer clearly separable, and when the distinctions between causes and effects begin to dissolve, individual responsibility becomes difficult to assign. As a result of this shift in emphasis, the past is no longer so fixed, the future no longer so predictable, and the mechanical expositions of formal realism no longer sufficient to explore the dynamic interplay of past and present. The sequential, linear, causal chain that connects past and present in Miller's early plays is subsumed, as his work matures, by an interacting, multi-linear, exploratory process: uncovering the process by which past is related to present *becomes* the process that the plays explore.

In order to accommodate this evolving notion of process, Miller has continually adapted the conventions of Ibsenian realism that first attracted him to playwriting. Like O'Neill, Wilder, and Williams, he has experimented with antimimetic devices and with the shape of dramatic form to make the equal reality of past and present equally apparent on the stage. He has not, however, abandoned his insistence on exploring causality and personal responsibility, and he constantly seeks to reconcile these interests with his interest in the complexity of relationships between past and present. As a result, the emphasis provided by Miller's dramatic structures has shifted throughout his career: at times he depends extensively on techniques of formal realism to illustrate the effects of given causes, but at other times he moves beyond these techniques so his characters can explore possible past causes for given present effects. His stage reality is indeed one where "consequences of actions are as real as the actions themselves," but the "reality" of both action and consequence turns out to be complex, shifting, and uncertain.

Formal Realism: The Question of Actions and Consequences

All My Sons (1947), Miller's first theatrical success, clearly demonstrates the centrality of the past to the Ibsenian stage world of Miller's early career. The play is constructed upon a rising sequence of revelations about Joe Keller and his relationship to his family. As the long-hidden secrets disclosed bit by bit throughout the play begin to fit together in a discernible causal chain, we learn that Keller had knowingly shipped out defective engine parts during the war and so is responsible for the deaths of twenty-one pilots; that he had allowed his business partner, still in prison as the play begins, to take the blame for the mishap; and that his older son, himself a pilot, had committed suicide after hearing of his father's possible involvement in the crime. The first two of these secrets have been kept hidden by Keller and his wife, the third by Ann, the dead son's fiancée. When all three secrets are exposed and the connections among them made apparent, Keller, unable to face the hideous consequences of his actions, follows his son in suicide. The play illustrates explicitly Miller's perennial theme of individual responsibility for even the unforeseeable effects of one's actions.

The structure of the play—which Miller has called "linear or eventual in that every fact or incident creates the necessity for the next"[4]—further manifests Miller's theme of the continual reeruption of the causal past and its consequences. In a more recent comment on the relationship between the theme of responsibility and the structure of his plays, Miller revises the notion of linear necessity, and the shift in emphasis in his comments indicates the shift of emphasis his plays would take. He says:

> I suppose by structure I always mean the same thing . . .—that's the existence of fate, or high probability, which means that when a man starts out to do what he intends to do, he creates forces which he never bargained for. . . . I think this is true of almost every play. And then he's got to relate himself to what the results of his actions were.[5]

The "necessity" with which causal realism condemns Joe Keller is here reduced to the less imposing "high probability," a reservation in judgment that Joe Keller was not permitted. For given the linear necessity that accurately describes the movmement of *All My Sons*, Joe Keller has no opportunity to "relate himself" to the results of his actions. The cause-and-effect chain has been forged long before the action of the play commences, and revelation of this chain, not character interpretation or understanding of it, becomes the central process of the play.

All My Sons is in many ways a standard Ibsenian thesis play. The earliest critics and reviewers of the play were quick to point out its similarities to *The Wild Duck*, in which one of two business partners is unjustly singled out and imprisoned for fraud, and in which the son of the ostensibly "innocent" partner, like Chris Keller, feels compelled to destroy the lie on which his father's life is based.[6] Furthermore, *All My Sons* employs a typically Ibsenian retrospective method, in which an ordinary domestic scene in act 1 is gradually disrupted by innuendo, and a domestic crisis erupts to reveal a fatal secret. Even the successive minor revelations that precipitate the eventual crisis are, like the damaging letter Ann withholds until the last act, stock devices of Ibsenian realism.

For Miller, however, the technical similarity to Ibsen was a minor corollary to their similarity of concern. According to Miller, his own interest consisted primarily in documenting the causal past and demonstrating its inexorable hold on the present. He says:

> *All My Sons* takes its time with the past, not in deference to Ibsen's method as I saw it then, but because its theme is the question of actions and consequences, and a way had to be found to throw a long line into the past in order to make that kind of connection viable.[7]

This comment suggests a double naïveté on the young Miller's part: he refused to see the connection between his self-proclaimed "linear" method and an Ibsenian thesis play, and he failed at this point in his career to see that more than a single line of causality must be established if "actions and consequences" are multiple, as his own use of the plural would suggest. By designing a structure to "bring a man into the direct path of the consequences he has wrought,"[8] Miller constructed a stage past limited to a single chain of events set in motion by a single moment of poor judgment. This simplified notion of the past in turn reduced the theme of the play to a simple moral lesson: the consequences of people's actions catch up to them. This is not to imply, of course, that *All My Sons* is not compelling theatre, nor to diminish its importance in helping the young playwright develop the notions of causation and the past that would evolve throughout his career and greatly enlarge his dramatic capabilities. But by constructing a dramatic method that is "linear," that casts "a long line into the past," Miller cut off the possibility of depicting the tangled interplay of forces, both external and internal, that combine to create the intricately woven and never completely explicable pasts his later characters grapple with.

Compounding the problem of this simplistic notion of what the past actually comprises is the fact that it is kept secret, concealed from the audience and unsuspected by many of the characters. Act 1 is two-thirds over before we are shown any indication that the Kellers' lives are only superficially smooth, and even then we catch only hints: Kate Keller's overreaction to her husband's playing "jailer" with the neighborhood boys, for example, or Keller's insistent question, "What have I got to hide?"[9] Act 1 ends with Keller's fearful speculation that the case will be reopened, and so Kate's curtain line—an admonition to Keller to "Be smart"—fuels our suspicions even further.

The effect of keeping Keller's crime hidden from the audience until the final moment of act 2 and of Ann's producing Larry's letter, for which we are totally unprepared, late in act 3, is to keep the audience in suspense. The "process" thus described by the play is not one of a character's "relating himself" to the consequences of his actions, but one of unearthing and exposing Keller's secret past—a process set in motion by Chris and Ann and externally imposed on Keller. Chris eventually forces his father to acknowledge his participation in the crime, but Keller, who assigns his family business a higher priority than his wider social responsibility, must struggle to see what he has done wrong. He cries out to Chris, "Who worked for nothin' in that war? When they work for nothin', I'll work for nothin. . . . Half the Goddam country is gotta go [to jail] if I go!" (1:125). Joe finally commits suicide not only because he has come to accept his responsibility for the pilots' deaths, but also because he cannot bear having disappointed Chris. A few minutes before his death he tells Kate: "I'm his father and he's my son, and if there's anything bigger than that I'll put a bullet in my head!" (1:120). Keller's awareness that his past actions have partially created the present is thus forced on him through external agents, and the audience is denied both prior knowledge of the truth and participation in Joe's coming to terms with it. Not until somewhat later in his career would Miller learn to substitute a character's gradual internal exploration and eventual self-revelation for this rather mechanical process of exposition.

Just as Keller's final vision of his guilt is pressed upon him by Chris, so do the social consequences of Keller's actions seem superimposed on the private, backyard world of the play. Critics have recurringly complained of this split between the personal and the public, the psychological and the social, the emotional and the intellectual in Miller's plays.[10] While Dennis Welland, speaking specifically about *Death of a Salesman,* is undoubtedly correct in feeling that "what is irritating about such criticism is its assured conviction that the mixture of social drama and personal tragedy is unintentional,"[11] the lack of unity that has bothered critics throughout Miller's career does intrude into the world of *All My Sons.* Of course, this issue is simply a variant of Miller's concern for actions and consequences: private actions can and often do have public consequences, and several of Miller's later plays explore in detail the relationship between character and community. But the linear, Ibsenian method of *All My Sons,* which ultimately demands Keller's confession, depends upon Keller's relationships with his wife, his sons, his business partner, and Ann; Miller's attempts to place Keller's crime in a larger social context are thus disruptive and tedious. This problem is illustrated plainly in the long first act that introduces a horde of functionless neighbors, in Chris Keller's self-aggrandizing monologues about the role he played in the war, and in Chris's insistence that his father confess his long-past complicity to the authorities.

The final problem with the play, however, is not that it accounts for more than one variety of motiviation—a laudable attempt, certainly, to create a complex stage reality—but that its linear method renders such potential complexity irrelevant. When the past is nothing more than an irrefutable secret, when the relationship between past and present is unremittingly causal, and when the central character cannot bear to acknowledge his own part in forming this chain of events exposed by others, the possibilities for expressing multiple motivations diminish. Joe Keller's story is essentially a familial one, and Miller's attempts to expand the repercussions of Joe's actions beyond the Keller's fenced-in yard are subverted by the unilinear structure of the play, which both prohibits personal exploration on Joe's part and restricts the establishment of a wider social context.

In Miller's later plays, the public and private centers of interest are much more subtly related—a development many critics seem reluctant to acknowledge. The problem was never one of too many threads to weave together, but of a structure too narrow to incorporate all the strands. In *The Crucible* (1953) and *A View from the Bridge* (1956), both predominantly formally realistic plays like *All My Sons*, Miller developed structural methods for demonstrating the presence of the past and the consequences of actions, while at the same time linking public effects of actions with private ones. By expanding one or two significant components of formal realism but preserving the general method, Miller opened up his stage to a more complex and compelling vision of the past's impact on the present.

The cause-and-effect structure that so severely limits the action of *All My Sons* provides the perfect framework for the relentless causality of *The Crucible*, in which each action has an immediate impact on those that follow. Like Joe Keller, John Proctor has committed a moral transgression in the past, his "lechery" with the servant girl Abigail. Unlike Keller, however, Proctor has admitted his wrongdoing to his wife Elizabeth, dismissed Abigail from their service, and attempted to restore order to his life. But Proctor's rejection of Abigail has set in motion a disastrous chain of events with multiple and widespread social consequences: Abigail's jealousy of Elizabeth leads her to accuse Elizabeth of practicing witchcraft; the accusation leads to Elizabeth's imprisonment; and the incarcerated Elizabeth's lie to the magistrates, intended to save John from sharing her punishment, conflicts with the confession he has already made and so results in his death sentence. The linear structure thus works in part because it mirrors the inflexible logic of the self-righteous magistrates and ministers who conduct the witchcraft trials and decide the Proctors' fates. These figures of authority are rather like the Tyrones of O'Neill's *Long Day's Journey into Night*, who interpret the mere temporal sequence of events as unavoidable causality and so absolve themselves of personal responsibility for the consequences of their actions. The causal movement these men wrongly discern, which the play's structure echoes, produces the "certain marching tempo" (as Sir Laurence Olivier called it)[12] that speeds the play to its inevitable conclusion.

Miller's treatment of the past in *The Crucible* is also more complex than that in *All My Sons*. Most obvious is that John's "lechery," unlike Keller's crime, is not kept hidden from the audience: although the other characters do not discover the sin until act 3, we spectators learn of John's shameful secret midway through act 1. Likewise, the future of the Salem characters is known to us through history, so we expect the deaths of many innocent townspeople. Because the past and future are thus apparent from the outset, the focus of attention can remain fixed on the process by which John Proctor "relates himself" to the consequences of his actions. By exposing the past early and predicting, by means of relentless causal structure and dramatic irony, the outcome of the events presented, Miller has provided a perspective that includes the cause-and-effect component of personal responsibility but also allows scope for exploring internal process. The surprise we feel as the secrets of *All My Sons* are revealed is here replaced by anticipation of the unavoidable future and participation in Proctor's exploration of his unfolding present.

The emphasis in this play is thus shared by two separate sorts of process: one that depicts actions and consequences, and one that shows what happens in the interval between those actions and their consequences. Through this second process, Proctor learns to accept public responsibility for the repercussions of even his most private actions. At the outset of the play, Proctor feels that his sinful "lechery" is a thing set apart in the private past, unconnected to the public present and no longer influential. The ensuing witchcraft trials, inspired primarily by the spiteful Abigail, soon disabuse him of this notion. That the events of the play enable Proctor to "relate himself" to the consequences of his actions is abundantly clear near the play's end, when Proctor is offered the chance to sign a confession of witchcraft and so be set free. But Reverend Parris's gloating as Proctor prepares to sign the confession reminds Proctor that his actions may have unforeseeable consequences; Parris declares, "It will strike the village that Proctor confess" (1:326). Heeding Parris's unwitting reminder of the possible public repercussions of his action, Proctor rejects their offer of life based on a lie (a sin that surely must have seemed, at first, inconsequential) and forestalls their plan to use his signing to condemn others. He declares:

> You will not use me! . . . I have three children—how may I teach them to walk like men in the world, and I sold my friends? . . . I blacken all of [those friends] when this is nailed to the church the very day they hang for silence! (1:327)

Once Proctor recognizes the communitywide effects that his single, private action of signing could produce, he can accept both the continuing influence of the past on the present and the social context in which even the most personal actions (a love affair, a lifesaving lie) reverberate. In Proctor, Miller has succeeded in linking the private and public worlds that remain unhappily separate in *All My Sons*, by showing how the individual error is replicated in the lives of others.

This mingling of private and public is made possible by the communal nature of the theocratic society in which Proctor lives. What Proctor does not realize at the outset of the play is that the guilt he feels about his "lechery" is shared in some form or another by each member of his demanding and unforgiving society, and that this omnipresent sense of guilt is what allows the witch-hunt hysteria to erupt. As Miller has said, "No man lives who has not got a panic button, and when it is pressed by the clean white hand of moral duty, a certain murderous train is set in motion."[13] The notion of the past important to this play includes the prior moral transgressions of the entire community and the whole moral framework that makes the notion of transgression so inevitable. Proctor's sin, therefore, is both a private failing and a representation of the repression endured by all his fellows. Guilt was no longer something for the playwright to expose, but something he could take for granted—his donnée. Miller says:

> It was no longer enough for me to build a play, as it were, upon the revelation of guilt. . . . Now guilt appeared to me no longer the bedrock beneath which the probe could not penetrate. I saw it now as a betrayer, as possibly the most real of our illusions, but nevertheless a quality of mind capable of being overthrown.[14]

The simple secret past of *All My Sons* is thus richly replaced in *The Crucible* by an entire network of prior sin and private guilt.

Because the community at large unwittingly engineers the "murderous train" from the start, the long, rather slow first act of *The Crucible* succeeds where that of *All My Sons* did not. Instead of simply introducing a backyard full of dramatically functionless neighbors to establish "an atmosphere of undisturbed normality,"[15] *The Crucible* begins with the illness of the apparently bewitched Berry Parris, the interrogation of the guilty Abigail about her hedonistic dancing, and the greedy squabbling of the townspeople over property and boundary lines. The townsfolk introduced so early in the action are clearly more than the "clutter of minor characters" that a number of critics object to:[16] as they crowd into Betty's bedroom, the citizens of Salem demonstrate the overpowering presence of the theocracy even in the most personal matters.

The emotional imprisonment imposed upon the characters by their theocracy and the relentless forward movement produced by the structure of the play are both represented visually in the play's four settings, each of which anticipates the Proctors' literal incarceration at the end. Act 1 takes place in Betty's clean but sparsely furnished attic room. The stage directions call for a crisscross, cagelike pattern of light and shadow, as sunlight streams across the room from the single narrow window at the left, and the exposed beams of the rafters loom close overhead. The Proctors' house, scene of act 2, is represented by "a low, dark, and rather long room," (1:261), typical of the time, but here emblematic of the theocratic systems of enclosure that are beginning to bear down on John and Elizabeth Proctor. The vestry room of the Salem meeting house provides the setting for act 3. "Now serving as the anteroom of the General Court" for the witchcraft trials, the room is described as "solemn, even forbidding" (1:285), as its high windows, symmetrical arrangement of plain furnishings, and jutting, heavy beams repeat the prisonlike imagery of act 1. Act 4, of course, takes place in an actual jail cell, in which the high barred window, simple benches, and streaks of moonlight seeping through the bars indicate how little the prison differs from the daily reality of the theocracy at large. Like the formally realistic structure of the play, the set itself reveals the inevitable results of the guilty terror that has long been smoldering in Salem.

In *The Crucible*, Miller was able—for the first and only time in those of his plays that are predominantly realistic—to explore simultaneously both his interest in actions and consequences and his interest in the process between them, by which Proctor comes to terms with the impact of his past choices on the present and the future. The importance of this shift in emphasis in Miller's work from given causality to constructed process is apparent in a comment of Miller's on *A View from the Bridge:* "It is not enough any more to know that one is at the mercy of social pressures; it is necessary to understand that such a sealed fate cannot be accepted."[17] From this point on in Miller's career, cause-and-effect relationships are not simply given but remain open to discovery and reinterpretation; no character's fate is sealed before he or she discovers it, for in the process of discovering it the individual helps constitute it.

Like *The Crucible*, *A View from the Bridge* presents events and their consequences in a structure not bound by the temporal limits of the play; like *The Crucible*, it focuses on a man who refuses to accept the sealed fate his past offers him. Eddie Carbone, an immigrant dock worker, violates his society's code of honor when he reports his wife's illegally immigrated cousins to the authorities. Although Eddie acts to protect his niece from an inappropriate suitor (and partly because he is unwittingly attracted to the niece himself), Eddie knows from the start what the inescapable consequences of his action will be: early in the first act he approvingly relates the story of a young man who was beaten up by his family and cast out by his community because he reported his uncle to the Immigration Bureau. That Miller was once again concerned with actions and their consequences is evident from his comments on the play:

The pressure of time's madness is reflected in the strict and orderly cause-and-effect structure of *A View from the Bridge*. Apart from its meaning, the manner in which the story itself is told was a rejection of the ennervated "acceptance" of illogic which was the new wisdom of the age. Here,

actions had consequences again, betrayal was not greeted with a fashiona-
bly lobotomized smile.[18]

The past that gives rise to this causal necessity, however, is no single
secret or past error, but the entire social code to which Eddie and his
peers subscribe. The play thus resembles *The Crucible* in its ability to
locate in one character's personal conflict the problems besetting the
community at large.

In *A View from the Bridge,* however, Miller adds yet another dimension to the personal and community conflicts that the play shares with
The Crucible. Through the presence of the lawyer Alfieri, who functions as both legal advisor to Eddie within the plot and as narrator for
the audience from outside the proscenium arch, Miller presents
causal sequence as something to be adjudicated, a task in which he
includes the audience by means of the lawyer's direct presentation of
Eddie's case. At the outset of the play Alfieri helps us see Eddie's
future actions in the context of a large historical perspective:

> In some Caesar's year, in Calabria perhaps or on the cliff at Syracuse,
> another lawyer, quite differently dressed, heard the same complaint and
> sat there as powerless as I, and watched it run its bloody course. (1:379)

With these words, Alfieri presents us with a vision of Eddie's past as a
social involvement he shares with generations of ancestors. He also
predicts the bloody outcome of the events we are about to witness.
Later he accelerates this play's version of that "certain marching
tempo," as he describes his first encounter with Eddie:

> I knew, I knew then and there—I could have finished the whole story that
> afternoon. It wasn't as though there was a mystery to unravel [as there had
> been in *All My Sons!*]. I could see every step coming, step after step, like a
> dark figure walking down a hall toward a certain door. (1:410)

With Alfieri's help we too can foresee the inevitable outcome of
Eddie's misguided passion. Alfieri's broadened perspective thus functions in much the same way as the historical time frame and resultant
dramatic irony do in *The Crucible:* the play's linear structure emphasizes separable causes and effects, but Alfieri's narrative interruptions
draw attention to the process that impels Eddie's decision and away
from the dreadful consequences we know to expect. As a result, the
audience feels anticipation rather than surprise, and prolonged adjust-

ment to the consequences of Eddie's actions replaces sudden resolution. Although Alfieri's narrative comments do somewhat disrupt the focus on Eddie, they allow us to know about and share in Eddie's decision-making process. In *A View from the Bridge*, Miller creates a balance between internal process and external causality, and allows the audience to participate in maintaining that balance.

Both *The Crucible* and *A View from the Bridge* demonstrate Miller's changing conception of the relationship between external causality and the inner processes by which characters come to recognize it. Both plays, however, provide only temporary structural solutions for this evolving notion of process. The auspicious combination of theme, historical perspective, and linear structure that *The Crucible* enjoys would be impossible to recapture in a modern context, and the device of the external narrator that extends the perspective in *A View from the Bridge* sits uneasily alongside the rest of the play's concentration on interior process. Both these plays succeed in demonstrating that actions have consequences for which the characters are responsible, and both depict part of the process by which the characters come to terms with this responsibility. But because of their essentially linear structure, both plays also present causal events as indisputable facts, not subject to reinterpretation during the central character's confrontation process. The past in these plays is entirely an objective set of experiences.

In Miller's later plays, pivotal past events are opened up for further exploration: they are often multiple, obscured from view, reconstructed and recreated by the characters' fallible memories. Past incidents become more than links in a chain of temporal causality, despite the characters' struggles to forge such a chain. In order to create a past more consistent with his evolving notion of ongoing process (and less dependent on a separable causal past and a predictable future), Miller had to de-emphasize linear realism and explore the mental processes of his characters in more detail. In *Death of a Salesman*, he did just that. As Miller says:

> Where in *All My Sons* it had seemed necessary to prove the connections between past and present, between events and moral consequences, between manifest and hidden, in [*Death of a Salesman*] all was assumed as proven to begin with.[19]

By taking the past's complex and multiple influence on the present for granted instead of striving to demonstrate a single, linear connection between past and present, Miller prepared his stage world for his greatest dramatic successes.

Death of a Salesman: A Mobile Concurrency of Past and Present

Willy Loman's past continually invades his present in *Death of a Salesman* (1949). As the play begins, we find Willy at a belated crossroads in his life, near retirement and unable to support his family, groping to understand the reasons for his failures as a father and as a salesman. Unknown to Willy, somewhere in his soul-searching he has lost track of the boundary between past and present. His first long speech demonstrates the collision of past and present in Willy's mind, as he conflates his present tale of driving his Studebaker with his memory of opening the windshield on the Chevy he used to own. As Miller has explained the germination of this character:

> The *Salesman* image was from the beginning absorbed with the concept that nothing in life comes "next," but that everything exists together and at the same time within us; that there is no past to be "brought forward" in a human being, but that he is his past at every moment and that the present is merely that which his past is capable of noticing and smelling and reacting to.[20]

It is clear from this statement that Miller had shifted his focus from disclosing the eternal facts of linear causal chains to depicting one character's attempt to locate them appropriately in his memory. The past thus portrayed in *Death of a Salesman* is one bound on all sides by the mind and imagination of Willy Loman.[21]

In order to dramatize this simultaneous existence of past and present in Willy's mind, Miller interrupts the present action of the play twice in each act with scenes from Willy's memory. Willy's recollections form a large part of his present reality; they influence his behavior as much as his current interactions with the other characters do. In order to portray this compelling inner world in all its potency, Miller chose to embody it on the stage and so demonstrate the present impact of Willy's private truths. Willy actually converses with his dead brother Ben, sometimes confusing Ben's voice with that of his neighbor Charley who is physically present in Willy's kitchen, and sometimes suppressing the world of external reality entirely to seek Ben's advice. He also recalls his son Biff's childhood adoration of him and the boy's triumph as a high school football hero. Most important, he relives his version of the single secret mistake that doomed Joe Keller and John Proctor, and which Willy fears has doomed him: his affair with a woman in Boston and the adolescent Biff's discovery of it. Early reviewers of the play (such as T. C. Worsley, William Beyer, and John Gassner—collected in Gerald Weales's edition) saw Willy's reliving of the past as a simple flashback, but Miller more accurately describes the technique:

> There are no flashbacks in this play but only a mobile concurrency of past and present, and this, again, because in his desperation to justify his life Willy Loman has destroyed the boundaries between then and now.[22]

To portray this intertwining of past and present in Willy's mind, Miller presents the scenes from the past expressionistically, in contrast to the external linear realism of the present action. Each time Willy's memories begin to overwhelm him, the lighting softens, the leaves of autumns past begin to fall, and the flute music of Willy's childhood begins to play, all unnoticed by the other characters but real to Willy and apparent to us. The young Linda and the adolescent sons who people Willy's imagination disregard the boundaries of realism, ignoring the wall lines of the fragile little house that both shelters and confines them in the present world. This alternation of expressionistic devices with those of formal realism in the play's structure enabled Miller both to explore and to portray visually that "friction, collision, and tension between past and present which was at the heart of the play's particular construction."[23]

Because we spectators observe this repeated "friction" between past and present, the focus of our attention is directed not toward ultimate causes, but to the process by which these causes are reviewed and recreated in Willy's groping mind. There is, of course, a characteristically Milleresque chain of causal events in Willy's past: it begins with Biff's discovery of Willy's infidelity, continues in the boy's subsequent refusal to finish high school or enter college, and finally results in the perpetual animosity between the two. But the process that Miller emphasizes here is twofold, including both Willy's attempt to "relate himself to what the results of his actions were" and also his equally important yet incompatible need to deny his part in causing

Biff's failures. The tension between given causality and reconstructed process is thus personified in Willy's psychological activity and becomes the very subject of the play as well as its method of development. Willy suspects that he is in part responsible for his own and his son's failures, but he cannot bear to face his responsibility squarely. He therefore retreats to his memory world in part to confront the truth that lies there and in part to escape the consequences of the past exposed by the linear present.

The causal past that Willy both seeks and fears to discover is unknown to us as the play begins, although we are given hints of it throughout act 1. The Boston woman's laughter from offstage (that is, from Willy's memory) counterpoints Linda's in the present, and the strain between Biff and Willy seems to spring from a hidden source that only the two of them know. But unlike Joe Keller, who carefully conceals his single, secret crime, Willy Loman simply refuses for most of the play to recognize the continuing consequences of his long-past affair. The past Miller discloses gradually throughout this play is thus part hidden and part obvious, part constructed by Willy, part ignored by him, and part discovered by him.

It is not until the second and last act that Bernard, a neighbor, unwittingly discloses the real reason that Biff refused to finish high school and in so doing forces Willy to acknowledge the part he played in Biff's failures. Bernard asks Willy why Biff had refused to enroll in the summer class that would have enabled him to attend college, and Willy answers:

> Why? Why? Bernard, that question has been trailing me like a ghost for the last fifteen years. He flunked the subject, and laid down and died like a hammer hit him!

But Bernard recognizes a different causality and replies:

> No, it wasn't right then. . . . He wasn't beaten by it at all. But then, Willy, he disappeared from the block for almost a month. And I got the idea that he'd gone up to New England to see you. Did he have a talk with you then? . . . What happened in Boston, Willy? (1 : 189–90)

It is only after Bernard forces Willy to recognize the impact of his infidelity on Biff that Willy can bear to remember the incident himself. In his very next retreat into his memory, Willy finally confronts what happened in Boston, and the causal link Willy has tried so desperately to hide from himself finally surfaces both on the stage and in his consciousness. We have not been duped here by a man hiding a crime (as we were by Joe Keller); instead, we share in the tortured mental processes by which Willy tries to forget the very truth he seeks and so evade responsibility for the consequences of his actions.

Willy Loman's failures extend beyond his shattered dreams for his son, however. Because Willy has never been able to realize his own dream of success in the business world, part of the self-exploring process Willy enacts for us has been precipitated by his own disappointment. Willy's preoccupation with his lackluster career, like his obsession with his son, colors both his present actions and his memories of the past: we see Willy seeking a raise and borrowing money in the realistic present of the play, and we overhear a conversation with Ben in Willy's memory, in which Willy rejects his brother's offer of adventure and wealth in favor of a career in sales.

Although Willy's failure to succeed financially as a salesman remains a mystery to him, the reasons soon become painfully obvious to us. Willy's skills are manual ones: he puts up a ceiling, rebuilds a stoop; as Charley says, "He was a happy man with a batch of cement" (1:221). But for Willy, it seemed that

> selling was the greatest career a man could want. Cause what could be more satisfying than to be able to go . . . into twenty or thirty different cities, and pick up a phone, and be remembered and loved and helped by so many different people? (1:180)

Willy craves membership in a large social world of successful businessmen, even while he resents the intrusion of the high-rise apartments and office buildings that accompany that world. Once again Miller has entangled the private, familial world of a character with that of his community. But in *Death of a Salesman* the problem of linking the two worlds is no longer just the playwright's, but the character's, as Willy seeks to reconcile his twin concerns for his career and his family.

What Miller has done in *Death of a Salesman* is invert his inquiries: instead of attempting to document the communitywide consequences of individual action (as he did in *All My Sons* and would do again, in part, in *The Crucible*), he explores the pressures of society at large on one individual member of it. In this way he maintains his focus on Willy's internal struggles to confront his past yet extends the implications of the chain of events that Willy finally constructs. By alternating scenes of externally valid causality with scenes of the random events Willy remembers, Miller demonstrates that:

> Society is inside of man and man is inside society, and you cannot even create a truthfully drawn psychological entity on the stage until you understand his social relations and their power to make him what he is and to prevent him from being what he is not. The fish is in the water and the water is in the fish.[24]

The past operative in Willy Loman's world thus extends far beyond Willy's unfortunate Boston indiscretion. As Miller would do again in microcosm in *The Crucible*, in *Death of a Salesman* he succeeded in implicating an entire society in the failures of one character. The past exposed in *Death of a Salesman*, then, comprises an entire network of private choices, public forces, and one man's remembered version of them. The play stands as a major milestone in the career of a playwright whose concept of the past develops from the making public of a single, secret crime to the making accessible an arena of privately constructed causalities and conflicting memories.

After the Fall and *The Price:* From Their Own Viewpoints

In *After the Fall* (1964) and *The Price* (1969), Miller continues the shift of emphasis begun in *Death of a Salesman* and accents the internal process by which a character "relates himself" to his past. A character's responsibility for the consequences of his or her actions is still a central theme, but the process of uncovering linear causality is now subsumed by the process of simultaneous internal and external exploration. Instead of trying to conceal or avoid present responsibilities for known past actions, each protagonist in these exploratory dramas seeks causes in his past to explain his present situation and help him chart a future course of action. For if there is one overriding change that sets these late plays apart from Miller's earlier works it is that the protagonists survive: we meet them not at the end of their lives (and at the end of a linear chain of events) but as they struggle with a crucial dilemma midway through them.

The process of deciding how to solve this dilemma determines the dramatic form of these late plays. They are structured not according to an externally verifiable causal sequence—which focuses attention on actions and consequences, beginnings and endings—but according to a character's interior reconstruction of one. This retrospective action is thus presented, as Miller said of the Franz brothers in *The Price*, "from their own viewpoints" (2:295).

That Miller's evolving notion of the past is central to his development as a playwright becomes evident in a comparison between the past set forth in *After the Fall* and that of the early *All My Sons*. Instead of the single, indisputable causal event guarded by Joe Keller in *All My Sons*, in *After the Fall* the past is a myriad and fragmented world of memories, with causal events yet to be discovered, interpreted, and evaluated, even by the one remembering. The central action of the play is the process by which Quentin investigates the remembered past and constructs and reconstructs causal sequences that permit him to understand and control his present. The focus is sharply set on the process of exploration, since causal events can be located only provisionally and proceed from a private viewpoint toward public acceptance rather than vice versa. As Quentin tells Maggie in the second act, "An event itself, dear, is not important; it's what you took from it" (2:214).

To permit this investigation of a past that contains few clearly discernible causal actions, Miller structured *After the Fall* according to the associations within Quentin's memory, and not to demonstrate temporal sequence or the overt consequences of actions. As the first line of the stage directions tells us, the action of the play takes place entirely "in the mind, thought, and memory of Quentin" (2:127). The set as Miller describes it resembles a human brain, with a "neolithic, a lavalike geography." Miller reminds us that "the mind has no color but its memories are brilliant against the grayness of the landscape." The actors in this play are the people of Quentin's memory, who "appear and disappear instantaneously, as in the mind," and so take their validity entirely from Quentin's perceptions. The overall effect Miller calls for is "the surging, flitting, instantaneousness of a mind questing over its own surfaces and into its depths." The only present action of the play is Quentin's ongoing dialogue with the unseen and unheard Listener, in which Quentin struggles to reach a decision about committing himself to a woman, Holga, whom he has recently grown to love. Every point in his decision-making process reminds him of past failures, of prior commitments he has failed to keep. In short, Quentin's decision-making process dictates both the subject and the structure of the play.

Late in the first act Quentin laments, "How few are the days that hold the mind in place; like a tapestry hanging on four or five hooks" (2:169). The hooks that support the fabric of his own memory are the moments of betrayal (both of him and by him) and the events which led up to them. He remembers his childhood and his mother's tricking him out of a vacation; he remembers walking out of his father's business when the old man most needed him. He remembers his infidelity to his first wife, and her subsequent tendency to blame all their marital failures on him alone. He remembers his relief at the suicide of his friend Lou, whose politically unpopular legal case Quentin had reluctantly taken on. Most of all he remembers the unhappily mixed motives that drew him and Maggie, his second wife, into marriage and led her eventually to suicide. The play thus reverses the emphasis of *Death of a Salesman*, as Quentin stumbles through the uncharted recesses of his memory in an attempt to discover the source of his failures and only occasionally returns to the single impending decision that locates him in the present and propels him into a future which Willy could not face.

Throughout the play, Quentin is engaged in the activity that killed Joe Keller, Willy Loman, and John Proctor: he is "relating himself to what the consequences of his actions were." Through the action of the play, Quentin comes to accept his responsibility for the effects of his actions, even if he is ignorant of them. Because Quentin feel that it is his responsibility to know, he feels "some vague . . . complicity" in any act of betrayal (2:148; ellipsis Miller's). Quentin's dilemma is to accept the burden of his life without being crippled by it, to kiss the idiot child in his arms (as Holga does in her dream), to forgive himself for living an imperfect life in an imperfect, post-Edenic world.

In order to do this, Quentin must undergo a Proctor-like jolt, a recognition and acceptance of even the unrealized yet possible consequences of his actions. Maggie's attempted suicide provides this jolt. Quentin at first tries to avoid taking any responsibility for his wife's desperation; he tells her, "the question is no longer whether you'll survive, but also whether I will" (2:228). He makes one last-ditch effort to force Maggie into becoming solely accountable for her own life and death. He tells her:

Do you see it, Maggie? Right now? You're trying to make me the one who does it to you? I take them [her sleeping pills]; and then we fight, and then I give up, and you take the death from me. You see what's happening? You've been setting me up for a murder. Do you see it? But I'm going away; so you're not my victim any more. It's just you, and your hand. (2:232–33)

Both Quentin and Maggie at this point are reversing the causal logic used by Miller's earlier characters: they are attempting to assign culpability on the basis of effect rather than of cause, and so to avoid acknowledging their part in creating the unintended consequences of actions. What Quentin comes to realize through his present exploration of this memory, however, is that even though he did not deliberately drive Maggie to suicide, and even though the responsibility for her action may rest ultimately with Maggie herself, he too must share a part of the blame for the despair that prompted her action.

Maggie's suicide attempt thus forces Quentin to acknowledge two things: his responsibility for even the unplanned and unforeseeable consequences of his actions, and the terrible mixture of motives, both innocent and guilty, that lurk in all human hearts. Because Quentin comes to see these mixed motives in his own relationship with Maggie, he learns to accept the responsibility he bears. In the final scene of the play he confesses the implications of his quarrel with Maggie; he tells the Listener:

Look, I'll say it. It's really all I came to say. Barbiturates kill by suffocation. And the signal is a kind of sighing—the diaphragm is paralyzed. [*With more difficulty.*] And I'd noticed it when we'd begun to argue. . . . I know, it usually does subside, but if not—each second can be most precious, why waste them arguing? What can be so important to gamble her life to get? [*The tower lights, fierce, implacable.*] My innocence, do you see? To get that back you kill most easily. . . . And her precious seconds squirming in my hands like bugs; and I heard. Those deep, unnatural breaths, like the footfalls of my coming peace—and I knew . . . I wanted them. (2:240)

What Quentin realizes here is that even in his own heart, "the wish to kill is never killed" (2:241); by learning about his past Quentin learns about himself and about society. The concentration camp tower that looms over the stage and over Quentin's memories lights up "implacably" at this point to unify Quentin's private version of complicity and the theme of universal guilt shared by the camp survivors. Early in the play Holga asserts that "no one they [the Nazis] didn't kill can be innocent again" (2:148). Quentin himself comes to share this vision of complicity in all acts of murder; he tells Maggie that "a suicide kills two people, Maggie. That's what it's for" (2:231). By surviving Maggie's suicide—and in fact, by inadvertently laying part of the foundation for it, just as some "innocent" stonemasons built the camp tower—Quentin shares Maggie's guilt, her human ability to kill.

Although a number of critics have failed to see the connections between Quentin's personal life and Nazi Germany,[25] these connections become abundantly clear to Quentin himself as the play progresses. Miller has used Quentin as a sort of central consciousness, a perspective from which we can view the relationship between a single character's human frailties and the larger evil in the world—a relationship that Proctor merely accepts, but Quentin explores. Quentin believes he has participated in Maggie's death. He also understands the political repercussions of private choices, as he confesses his fear of being known as a "Red lawyer" because he has defended Lou. From this Proctor-like recognition of the interaction between private actions and public effects, it is no large step for Quentin to feel a "vague complicity" with the Germans who built the concentration camp he and Holga visited. At the moment when he confesses his relief at Lou's suicide—"the joy I felt now that my danger had spilled on the subway track"—Quentin admits that the concentration camp and all it stands for "is not some crazy aberration of human nature to me" (2:184). Quentin's journey through his past finally enables him to embrace his guilt-ridden life and all its fundamentally human sins (as Proctor eventually does), and to allow Holga's love to help him forgive it.

The presence of the unseen Listener underscores these central connections between private actions and social responsibility. In Miller's early plays the causal past was objectively verifiable, a matter of public record—as attested by the presence of the narrator Alfieri in *A View from the Bridge* or the long historical narrations in *The Crucible's* stage directions. In *After the Fall*, however, Quentin creates his own version of the past and must subject it to the public testing that requires the presence of the Listener. If we as audience are to be equated with the Listener (as his imaginary presence in our midst would indicate), we provide the social context for Quentin's reconstruction of the past, and we are implicated in the conclusions he draws. It is no coincidence that Quentin, like Alfieri, is a lawyer, determined to follow legal procedures. But whereas Alfieri sought our agreement with a decision already handed down, Quentin seeks our judgment on the provisional causality he is investigating and on the notion of universal human guilt he is striving to apply to his own case. The Listener thus indicates the priority of public responsibility in this play, despite the structural focus on private vision by which that responsibility can be recognized.

After the Fall received an overwhelmingly unfavorable critical reception, due in large part to its adherence to Quentin's interior logic. Perhaps in response to this negative criticism, Miller shifted his emphasis in *The Price* to include more of the formal realism of his earlier plays. *The Price* is a rather austerely constructed play, with only four characters, unity of time, and the single naturalistic setting of an attic room cluttered with a lifetime's accumulated junk. But *The Price* does share an important assumption with the wider-ranging, more impressionistically constructed *After the Fall:* it assigns dramatic priority to the interior logic of individual hindsight, which alone can assign causality to past events. By thus combining formally realistic characters and staging with a retrospective plot based on interior notions of causality, Miller created the unique and concentrated power of *The Price.*

There is very little conventional action in *The Price,* and the dramatic situation is simple. Victor and Walter Franz, a police patrolman and an eminent surgeon respectively, meet after sixteen years of estrangement to sell the contents of their long-dead parents' recently condemned house. The memories stirred up by their uncomfortable reunion force each man to reassess his understanding of the past events that in part created the present. What little present "action" the play includes is thus largely retrospective: either the characters analyze and explore the past through dialogue (as Victor and his wife Esther do in the opening minutes), or they unknowingly recapitulate it (as Victor and Walter do in responding to Solomon, who comes to represent their father as he sits in the old man's center-stage chair).

The connections between actions and their consequences that Miller once struggled to illustrate are all taken for granted in *The Price,* as once again the playwright's former dramatic problems become personal problems for his characters. Each of the characters acknowledges, in one form or another, what Victor asserts in act 1: "You've got to make decisions before you know what's involved, but you're stuck with the results anyway" (2:237). What Victor himself does not at this point realize is that the decision-making process itself is at best an illusory one, that the moment he remembers so vividly as pivotal has undergone gradual reconstruction in his memory. The decision he made to support his father during the Depression instead of continuing his own education seems to him now to have been unavoidable. But as the play progresses Victor is forced to acknowledge that his conviction that he "had to drop out to feed the old man" is not entirely justifiable. As Walter points out, the expensive golden harp that dominates the downstage area provides ample proof that their father was never destitute. The problem explored in *The Price*, then, is not so much one of relating actions to consequences, but of recogizing that causal incidents themselves are endlessly debatable, fixed only provisionally by individual memory. What had seemed like a solution in *After the Fall* becomes the central problem of *The Price*.

Miller is able to explore the complex connection between memory and causality in *The Price* because the present action is so minimal. Unlike *After the Fall*, in which Quentin's queries derive their urgency from the present decision he must make, in *The Price* both actions and their consequences, both causes and their effects, are relegated to the past. Victor's decision to drop out of college has had its results in his unfulfilling and financially unrewarding career as a policeman. Walter's decision to leave home and pursue his medical degree has also shown its eventual consequences in financial security, accompanied by a divorce and a nervous breakdown. Each brother has paid the price for his choice. What is left to investigate is the process by which those choices were originally made. Miller in this way uses present process (Victor's growing recognition that his remembered truths are partial ones) as a structural principle to explore thematic process (how the brothers first made the decisions they now see as causal). By beginning in the present and moving backward into the past, *The Price* reverses the linearity of Miller's earlier plays and completes the shift in emphasis from unforeseen effects to unfixable causes that has grown throughout his career.

The conflict between the two brothers is not primarily one of present tensions, but of the incompatible visions by which they have structured their mutual past. After his hospitalization, Walter feels he has gained a new insight into his brother. He feels that his own breakdown occurred over a period of time, as a result of social pressures and obligations. He says: "It all happens so gradually. . . . You become a kind of instrument, an instrument that cuts money out of people, or fame out of the world" (2:350). But despite Walter's belief that his own fate emerged gradually, he sees Victor's as the result of a conscious, causal decision: "You see," he tells Victor, "it never dawned on me until I got sick—that you'd made a choice. . . . You wanted a real life. And that's an expensive choice; it costs" (2:350–51). But Victor's version of the past is quite different. For him, Walter deserted the family and refused to help his brother with tuition money. Like Walter, Victor feels himself to be the victim of time and circumstances, and he sees Walter as the one who made a choice. He refutes Walter's version by saying, "I didn't invent my life. Not altogether. You had a responsibility here and you walked on it" (2:363).

The truth of the matter is that Victor has, in large part, reinvented his own past—as all four of the characters have. When Walter implies that Victor knew all along that their father had some hidden savings, Victor cries out, "I don't know what I knew" and *his voice and his words surprise him* (2:365). In the light of Victor's growing awareness, Walter's words ring true when he says, "We invent ourselves, Vic, to wipe out what we know. You invent a life of self-sacrifice, a life of duty; but what never existed here cannot be upheld" (2:369). Through the conflict with Walter, Victor discovers that the familial love he protected at the cost of his own future was an illusion. He forces himself to remember that loss of the family fortune caused the breakup of the family. But in the process of facing this other possible truth about his past and its influence on his present life, Victor discovers in himself a set of values uniquely his. As Miller puts it, "In *The Price* a man is faced with the fact that he participated in his own alienation from himself and in so doing discovers himself in what he did."[26]

In *The Price*, then, Miller has moved well beyond his original notion of actions and consequences. *The Price* is, rather, an epistemological drama, exposing the processes by which the characters "know what they know," and exploring the limited influence of objective facts upon the lives the characters construct for themselves. The play seems to echo Victor's haunting question, "What's the difference what you know?" when the structuring of all experience depends upon something as fragile as memory.

Because there can be no conclusive answer to the questions of what we know and how we know it, *The Price* can have no formal resolution. Walter's construction of his own life's truths has been as illusory and as valid as Victor's. As the opening stage directions tell us, "A fine balance of sympathy should be maintained in playing the roles of Victor and Walter. . . . As the world now operates, the qualities of both brothers are necessary to it" (2:295). This equilibrium essential to the play's theme is reflected in its structure: if the present action consists primarily of retrospective exposition, then no forward movement—no resolution or denouement—is possible. Miller's interest in process finally, in *The Price*, pulls him away from his old insistence on discovering unquestioned causal events in the past and plunges his characters into the world of individually designated causes and inwardly verifiable knowledge. As Miller has said, "A genuine work of art creates not completion, but a sustained image of things in tentative balance."[27] All that is left for the Franz brothers to do is to continue on the paths they now know they have blazed for themselves.

A Highly Condensed Interior Life

Arthur Miller's literary career has been much more varied than my analysis in terms of causation and process might suggest. His work to date includes a novel, an adaptation of an Ibsen play, several one-act plays, a number of screenplays, a collection of short stories, and a comic drama. But time and again throughout his career Miller has returned to his interest in dramatizing process, in discovering the ways in which characters discover the seeds of their present in the soil of their past.

Miller's recent work continues many of these patterns. In *The Archbishop's Ceiling* (1984), for example, Miller returns to the problem of how we know what we know. The play explores the relationships between a group of writers and an actress in a politically repressive country, who fear (but never know for certain) that their conversations are being monitored by a device hidden in the baroque ceiling. We can see Miller's characteristic concerns: guilt, responsibility, and the illusory quality of our knowledge. And as Welland describes the play's structure, "the whole play is exposition, for it involves virtually no action and there is no denouement in any tidily conventional sense."[28] Exposition, however, also becomes complication, for in Miller's stage world it no longer exists as an indisputable set of given facts.

The problematic status of the past is also the subject of *Danger:*

Memory! (1986), which comprises two separate one-act plays loosely related by the theme of memory. In the first, *I Can't Remember Anything*, the past is the recurring topic of conversation—as well as dispute—between two elderly friends, each of whom remembers different details about their mutual past. *Clara*, the second and more interesting play in the volume, explicitly links the workings of memory to an individual's feelings of guilt. The action takes place in the darkened apartment of the murdered Clara Kroll, as a police detective questions her father, Albert Kroll, about his daughter's acquaintances. Clara was most probably murdered by her current lover, a Puerto Rican man who had served ten years in prison for murdering his former girlfriend. Kroll, however, has difficulty remembering the man's name.

Kroll's memory is blocked because of the guilt he feels. Clara's death is undoubtedly a result of her career as a dedicated social worker. She lived in an unsavory neighborhood, worked rehabilitating prisoners, and had recently been held hostage in an inmate riot. Now that Clara is dead, probably at the hands of her lover and former client, Kroll recalls all the encouragement he had given Clara and the obvious pride he had felt in her independence and public spirit. He recalls telling her stories about his own life—about the Negro platoon he had volunteered to command in the army and his championing the minority cause on the local zoning board—and suspects that his influence led her, eventually, to her death. "I wonder if I should ever have told her that story," he muses now.[29]

Because Kroll, like Quentin of *After the Fall*, feels some complicity in a loved one's death, he is unable to remember much of the past; he simply cannot face the truth about the unforeseen consequences of his actions. What facts he can remember appear in flashes, both to Kroll and to us, as Clara's darkened apartment is occasionally illuminated "for a subliminal instant" with "an exploding flash" of light (32). This technique, reminiscent of Williams's screen device in *The Glass Menagerie*, makes the flashes of memory an actual experience for the audience as well as for Kroll. "I can't understand why I'm seeing it like on a screen . . ." ponders the bemused Kroll (57). The detective, however, understands the workings of memory somewhat better; "We block things we're ashamed to remember," he tells Kroll (47).

In Kroll's case, at least, the detective is undoubtedly correct, for many happier memories of Clara are alive in Kroll's memory. At several points during the questioning Kroll remembers an endearing trait of Clara's—her fondness for animals, or her love for her fellow humans—and in each case the remembered Clara enters the scene, alive and visible both to Kroll and to the audience. This technique demonstrates the equal reality of past and present in Kroll's momentarily disordered mind, as Clara takes stage center at her own murder investigation. Like Willy Loman, however, Kroll has difficulty accepting his own past role in engineering his child's fate. It is only through his last monologue, a speech in which he remembers telling the sympathetic young Clara about some victims of racial prejudice, that Kroll finally faces the truth and recalls her lover's name. The process by which Kroll relates himself to the consequences of his past choices is all enacted before the audience; we participate in the vivid, fitful workings of his memory, becoming gradually aware that the past both determines and partially constitutes the present.

This discussion of the presence of the past in Miller's recent work highlights Miller's similarities to O'Neill and to other American playwrights. For although Miller's plays generally maintain more of stage realism than those of his compatriots, he does experiment with dramatic form in many of the same ways, and for many of the same reasons. Like O'Neill, Miller has restructured dramatic form to construct plays that are exploratory in nature, that reach no conventional conclusion, and that include or implicate the audience in the action. Like Wilder, he uses a narrator when he needs to invoke historical patterns or suggest the future significance of an action; lately, in *The American Clock* (1982), he even borrowed Wilder's technique of quick, onstage wig changes to illustrate the characters' moving back and forth in time. And like Williams, he uses antimimetic devices of all sorts to assert the equal reality of memory on an otherwise realistic stage.

Miller has, however, left a personal imprint on the shape of American drama and has extended the boundaries of the past in unique and valuable ways. By returning repeatedly to the theme of actions and consequences and by continually attending to structural methods for exploring process, Miller shows the impact of the past on the present to be less a fact to be disclosed and more a network of possibilities to be investigated. As a result, the structures of Miller's plays move away from linear realism and toward, as Miller describes it, "a realistic recognition of events and characters on the surface of a highly condensed interior life" (2:1). Miller's best and most enduring plays have been those (like *Death of a Salesman*, *The Crucible*, and *The Price*) in which exploring the past forms the central action of the present and in which the struggle to understand "that highly condensed interior life" means as much as and at times more than the outcome of events.

5

Tennessee Williams
Memory and the Passing Moment

Flora Goforth, the indomitable heroine of *The Milk Train Doesn't Stop Here Any More*, speaks for most of Tennessee Williams's characters when she says:

> Has it ever struck you, Connie, that life is all memory, except for one present moment that goes by so quickly you hardly catch it going? It's really all memory, Connie, except for each passing moment.[1]

The obsession with memory that leads Flora Goforth to spend her days frantically dictating her memoirs is shared, in one form or another, by most of Williams's principal characters. Whether they attempt to escape their memories, recreate the past in the present, change the past to conform to the present, or control the present by controlling the accepted version of the past, Williams's major characters recognize memory as a repository of past truth and a powerful component of the present.

Despite this interest of Williams's characters in selectively arresting time in their memories, however, time does pass around them, and neither their present circumstances nor the moments seemingly suspended in their memories can avoid being affected by its passage. Although the characters often attempt to use memory as a barrier against the changes that time brings, they are also aware of time's unstoppable forward movement. Many of them share the fears of "One" in *I Can't Imagine Tomorrow*, who says:

105

> If there wasn't a thing called time, the passing of time in the world we live
> in, we might be able to count on things staying the same, but time lives in
> the world with us and has a big broom and is sweeping us out of the way,
> whether we face it or not.[2]

Time thus passes on Williams's stage at two different speeds: that
held steady in the characters' memories, and that moving forward in
the passing present moment. Much of the power of Williams's best
plays is generated by this conflict between the suspended moment of
memory and the sweeping broom of time.

As this central conflict indicates, Williams's dramatic interests are
related to those of Thornton Wilder, who struggled to portray "two
times at once." For Williams, however, the essential conflict is not
between the vast backdrop of historical time and the limited perspective of a single lifetime (as it was for Wilder), but between interior
time selectively arrested by memory and time that moves forward,
measured by clocks and calendars. To express this conflict, Williams
characteristically juxtaposes contrasting elements on the stage: realistically drawn characters embroiled in sequential plots move among
the antimimetic formal devices that Williams uses to depict their
memories.[3]

Williams recognized early in his career that the structures of formal
realism limited a playwright's ability to explore the interior reality of
his characters. In his now famous "Production Notes" to *The Glass
Menagerie,* Williams asserted the importance of these inner visions and
the need for a "plastic theatre" to express them. He claimed that

> truth, life, or reality is an organic thing which the poetic imagination can
> represent or suggest, in essence, only through transformation, through
> changing into other forms than those which were merely present in ap-
> pearance. (1:131)

Williams's continued attention to his characters' memories—the most
persistently significant aspect of their lives "not merely present in
appearance"—led him to develop a full repertoire of antimimetic
devices, including memory structure, episodic dream structure,
lengthy monologues, a play-within-a-play, and the clusters of mood-
setting music, antimimetic lighting, and visual symbols that enable
him to stage the inner visions of his characters. Williams did not,
however, discard formal realism entirely, nor did he abandon the
realistic handling of chronological time. Although he clearly sym-

pathized with his beleaguered characters' use of memory as a way of "snatching the eternal out of the desperately fleeting" (2:262), he was also fully aware that "the diminishing influence of life's destroyer, time, must be somehow worked into the context of his play" (2:263). The characters themselves, like Flora Goforth, are primarily interested in the validity of memory, but the playwright places equal emphasis on those "passing moments" of external time that Flora so offhandedly dismisses.

This conflict between remembered time and actual time recurs continually throughout Williams's career, although the emphasis between them shifts: some plays stress the potency of memory's inner truths, while others focus on memory's inability to halt time permanently. The principal combatants of Williams's stage world remain the same, however, as the playwright perennially explored the power of memory in a world where "the monosyllable of the clock is Loss, loss, loss, unless you devote your heart to its opposition" (1:141). And despite the vicissitudes of his critical reputation and the uneven quality of the plays within his canon, Tennessee Williams has left a profound mark on the modern theatre, an imprint produced largely by the "plastic" devices he used to explore the effects of memory's arrested vision on characters caught up in the relentless forward thrust of time.

The Scene Is Memory

In an essay entitled "The Past, the Present, and the Perhaps," Williams described his early work, *Battle of Angels*, as "a lyrical play about memories and the loneliness of them" (3:223). And indeed, this first major full-length play shows evidence of both Williams's devotion to the theme of memories and his reliance on technical experiments to explore those memories on the stage. The entire play, about the deaths of the two protagonists, Myra and Val, is told in a flashback by the gossiping Temple sisters. Within this flashback framework, the memories of the protagonists themselves are embodied on the stage, first in Myra's redecorated confectionery, replete with dogwood and other symbols of spring, youth, and innocence, and later by the arrival of a woman from Waco, whose accusations bring about Val's death. The original production of the play closed abruptly after an abbreviated Boston tryout, evidently failing to convince its spectators of the reality of those lonely memories. But *Battle of Angels* was to have two important repercussions in Williams's career. First, Williams eventually reworked the play into the more successful *Orpheus Descending*, in which the superimposed memory framework is dropped, the confectionery comes to represent specific events rather than innocence in general, and Val's demise is the direct result of his relationship with a central character instead of with a "villain ex machina" from Waco. Second, and more important, Williams re-designed the memory structure and integrated it closely with the thematic concerns of his next play, *The Glass Menagerie*.

Because "the scene is memory" (as Williams's stage directions indicate—1: 143), the action of *The Glass Menagerie* unfolds entirely as remembered by Tom Wingfield, who functions both as a narrator outside the proscenium arch and as a character within its confines. The memory framework that seemed superimposed on the story of Val and Myra is thus perfectly appropriate to *The Glass Menagerie*, since the one remembering is a central agent in the events he remembers, and the effects of those memories on him is a principal subject of inquiry. Furthermore, a central theme of *The Glass Menagerie* is the continued vitality of the past within one's memory, and Tom's con-struction of a memory play to explore the consequences of his mother's and Laura's unchanging memories on his own and Laura's changing lives dramatizes this theme effectively.[4]

The remembered past is clearly of primary importance not only to Tom the reminiscing narrator, but also to his mother, Amanda Wing-field, a central focus of Tom's memories. Amanda's memories of her aristocratic upbringing in Blue Mountain dominate the dialogue in the early scenes of the play and precipitate the action in the later ones. In scene 1, Amanda recalls the apparent high point of her youth: the afternoon that seventeen eligible gentlemen came to call on her. This evidently oft-repeated memory completely overwhelms the Wing-fields' present action of eating dinner: not only is Amanda's mono-logue uninterruptable, but it is highlighted (in the text, if not in the original production) by a slide screen in the Wingfield living room that flashes images of young Amanda and lines from Villon's "Ballade des dames du temps jadis." The tyranny of Amanda's memories over her own life and over the lives of her children is thus established with a striking antimimetic gesture at the outset of the play, and the im-plausibility of these memories does not diminish their ability to influence and even to constitute present action.

The impact of Amanda's memories on Laura becomes apparent in scene 2, in which Laura reveals her own cherished memories of a boy she had liked in high school. Laura's recited recollections, like those of her mother in scene 1, are accented by slides. These memories of her past—her crush on Jim and her painful shyness with him—lock Laura as securely into the world of the past as her mother's memories of gentlemen callers and her narrator-brother's memories of Laura herself do them. And once again, the external truth of the past exerts less influence and is of less importance than the emotional truth of Laura's memories. We find out later from Jim that he had never even noticed Laura's limp, but the clumping of the brace she used to wear echoes loudly in Laura's memory, undermining her self-confidence and limiting her chances for meaningful present activity.

Amanda's memories of her beaux and Laura's memories of Jim coalesce in the final scenes of the play, when the gentleman caller that Tom reluctantly brings home for Laura turns out to be none other than Jim himself. As Tom describes him, Jim is "the most realistic character in the play, being an emissary from the world of reality that we were somehow set apart from" (1:145). As such, Jim belies the present validity of the Wingfields' inner visions of the past: unlike the high-school hero that Laura remembers, Jim six years later is still a lowly factory clerk; unlike the prospective husbands who still call on Amanda in her memory, Jim is engaged to marry another girl. The stabilized reality of Laura's memory cannot withstand the shock of what the past has become in the present. When she discovers that passing time has destroyed her remembered truths and made impossible her remembered dreams, Laura retreats within herself forever.

For Tom, however, memory has a very different function. Unlike his mother and sister, Tom sees clearly the price they all have paid for failing to adjust their remembered truths to their changing present circumstances. Tom alone is willing to acknowledge that truth created and maintained in memory, albeit powerful and real, is not necessarily consistent with the external facts of the past or with their present manifestations. For this reason Tom separates his present self from his remembered self to function as a narrator, distanced in time and space, of the play-within-a-play of his memories. His comments as narrator indicate his awareness that his memories are selected and abridged; his presence in between the audience and the play itself suggests that his controlling vision has created a remembered reality largely independent of outside verification. As Williams asserts in the stage directions:

> The scene is memory and therefore nonrealistic. Memory takes a lot of poetic license. It omits some details; others are exaggerated, according to the emotional value of the article it touches, for memory is seated predominantly in the heart. (1:143)

The unconventional form of the play thus represents Tom's memory of the events rather than the events themselves: the episodic structure of the scenes, the dim lighting, the background music, and the screen device all portray the action as Tom remembers and interprets it. The causal sequences of formal realism certainly operate in the play—Amanda's potent memories and the persistent demands she makes on her children are the direct causes of both Laura's crippling introversion and Tom's eventual defection—but these causal sequences are obscured by the antimimetic symbols that illuminate the story in Tom's memory.

In *Vieux Carré*, written over thirty-five years after *The Glass Menagerie*, Williams returns to the memory form in another play, like *Battle of Angels*, about the loneliness of memories. This time, however, memory conflicts not with chronological and historical time as it did in *The Glass Menagerie*, but with death itself, the end result of time, against which memory can provide only a temporary shelter. Because chronology is not an issue here, there are no clearly delineated causal sequences in *Vieux Carré*. Rather, the play proceeds in fragmented flashes as the Writer (who narrates the play, as Tom Wingfield did, from outside the proscenium arch) remembers the people of his past and the uses to which they put their own remembered truths.

The play takes place within the Writer's memory of his few months' sojourn at a seedy rooming house in New Orleans's French Quarter, a house peopled by a tubercular artist, a dying fashion designer and her drug addict boyfriend, two old bag women, and an emotionally unbalanced landlady. Each of these inhabitants is desperately lonely, since they all live more in their individual memories than in their present actions, and each is slipping rapidly down the solitary road toward death as the Writer briefly enters their ranks. In order to avoid their solitary despair, these characters reach out to one another, and in the moments when they share their memories—and so include these memories in the realm of the present—they come closest to escaping the essential isolation that reminds them all of death. The Writer's memory of being seduced by a paratrooper opens the way for his relationship with the painter; the landlady's confusion of the Writer with her long-lost son Timmy enables the two to develop an almost familial closeness; and Jane's reminiscing about her first meeting with Tye reunites the lovers after a quarrel. To the characters, at least, memory thus beocmes a repository of inner truth and a means of communicating with others. This interaction between stabilized memory and fluid time provides a bond with life even in the shadow of approaching death.

The interaction between memory and present reality produces only a temporary relief, however. In the second half of the play the painter is removed to a charity hospital to die, Jane learns of her fatal disease, and Tye resumes his affair with the needle. So while "Part One" depicts the vitality of memory and its importance in creating a meaningful present, "Part Two" demonstrates death's inevitable victory over it. Death, however, does not have the last word in the play. The characters' memories may have provided only the impermanent solace of a bond with other human beings, but the presence of the Writer remembering them from outside the world of the action rescues the play from making the potentially banal point that memory dies along with the rememberer. The Writer remembers them all, and by means of his narration and his play, so do we. The paradox that death defeats memory but that memory, once shared and so incorporated into the present, can persist beyond individual death, is embodied in the memory structure of the play.

The form and staging both demonstrate the persisting reality of the Writer's memory: Williams calls for a multilevel playing area, minimal furnishings, episodic alternation of scenes, and the flickering, isolating spotlights of a remembering mind. The Writer's final comment to the audience underscores the unique vitality of memory, which can preserve things that life and death kill. He says about the characters of his play:

> They're disappearing behind me. Going. People you've known in places do that: they go when you go. The earth seems to swallow them up, the walls absorb them like moisture, remain with you only as ghosts [*sic*]; their voices are echoes, fading but remembered.[5]

Although "people you've known in places" cease to exist for you beyond the time and place in which you knew them, their reality is preserved in memory, and so, in a way, memory defeats the death that existence apart from memory must surely bring. Memory is thus presented as both a temporary barrier against the broom of time and an alternative reality where its sweep cannot be felt; it provides a way to connect past truths with present reality and so defeat the encroachment of time.

These two memory plays served important functions in shaping Williams's career: *The Glass Menagerie* made him an overnight celebrity, and *Vieux Carré* breathed promising new life into a career that many critics saw as finished in the 1960s. But the form of a memory play created certain problems for Williams as well. Although the presence of the narrator reconstructing his past asserts that remembered truths are an essential component of the present, the separation of narrator in the present from character in the past prohibits any complex interaction between the two. Since we witness no present action of the narrator's other than his act of remembering, we cannot know how his present circumstances may be affecting his reconstruction of the past, or how that past has helped shape his relatively undefined present situation. In order to explore more fully this interaction between time as it is remembered and time as it passes, Williams experimented with a number of other structural devices, including a play-within-a-play in which the characters themselves, not an external narrator, are intermittently self-conscious. Several other structural experiments, however, preceded Williams's return to the memory play-within-a-play—experiments that worked well by themselves in early plays and in turn informed later ones. One such method is the extended expository monologue, accompanied by the formal changes that occasionally allow it to become central to the drama.

Nothing Not Spoken

The expository monologue is an ancient device: one thinks of Creon's opening speech in *Antigone*, Othello's description of winning Desdemona's love, and many similar examples. In Williams's hands, however, like those of O'Neill before him, the monologue becomes more than a body of information to be conveyed. In Williams's plays the extended monologue acquaints us with the characters' internal visions of the past—much as the memory framework did in *The Glass*

Menagerie—and enables us to share the reality of these visions even though the external facts of the past may prove incompatible with them.

This technique works particularly successfully in *A Streetcar Named Desire*, in which the continuing influence of Blanche's memories and perceptions must be demonstrated, even though the actions and perceptions of the other characters often contradict them. In the following speech, Blanche explains to Stella how the family estate was lost:

> I, I, *I* took the blows in my face and body! All of those deaths! the long parade to the graveyard! . . . You just came home in time for the funerals, Stella. And funerals are pretty compared to deaths. . . . Unless you were there at the bed when they cried out "Hold me!" you'd never suspect there was the struggle for breath and the bleeding. You didn't dream, but I saw! *Saw! Saw!* And now you sit there telling me with your eyes that I let the place go! How in hell do you think all that sickness and death was paid for? . . . Why, the Grim Reaper had put up his tent on our doorstep! . . . And I with my pitiful salary at the school. Yes, accuse me! Sit there and stare at me, thinking I let the place go! *I* let the place go? Where were *you?* In bed with your—Polack! (1 : 261–62)

In this speech Blanche reveals more than just the outward truth of her family's dying out or the loss of the aptly named Belle Reve. Her horror at the reality of death, her resentment of what she perceives as Stella's disloyalty, her sense of guilt, and her defensiveness all emerge in this single speech. The images that Blanche uses to describe the deaths which haunt her indicate her melodramatic, rather Gothic turn of mind; her concluding accusation of Stella hints at the preoccupation with sexuality that drove Blanche from Laurel and will contribute to her eventual breakdown. The strident repetition of "I" and "saw" emphasizes the potency of Blanche's interior point of view; when combined with the plethora of exclamation marks that produce the speech's stacatto effect, this repetition reveals the brittleness beneath Blanche's cool white facade and predicts the emotional snap which will end her visit to her sister. Through the monologue we become acquainted with Blanche's idiosyncratic perception of past events and their relationship to present truths. Their validity in terms of what actually happened matters less than their continuing effect on all the characters as the action of the play commences.

In *Streetcar,* as I will discuss below, the values Blanche chooses to preserve in her memory are no longer operative in the world of the play, and her extended monologues function primarily to defend the present validity of those values in her own mind. In *Cat on a Hot Tin Roof,* however, Williams uses the extended monologue not just to assert the validity of memory, but to examine its capacity to change as time passes. The first fifteen pages of the text comprise Maggie's one-sided conversation with her husband Brick, who interrupts only occasionally with a sardonic comment. Her speech both exposes the past and elicits our sympathy for Maggie's point of view. For Maggie, however, holding on to a personal vision of the past is not enough; that vision must be adjusted to what the past has become in the present. Midway through act 1 she tells Brick:

> When something is festering in your memory or your imagination, laws of silence don't work, it's just like shutting a door and locking it on a house on fire in hopes of forgetting that the house is burning. But not facing a fire doesn't put it out. Silence about a thing magnifies it. It grows and festers in silence, becomes malignant. (3:31)

Maggie recognizes that when memory is used to preserve an unchanging, sacred past (as Brick has used it to enshrine the memory of his dead friend Skipper), its influence on the changing present can only be destructive. Maggie thus survives where Blanche does not because she confronts and adapts her own memories (of Brick, of Skipper) to conform to the demands of the present.

This adaptation is reflected structurally as well as thematically. Whereas Blanche speaks in extended monologues throughout *Streetcar* to assert the reality of her own inner vision, by the end of *Cat on a Hot Tin Roof* Maggie speaks primarily in dialogue with the other characters. Furthermore, Maggie's final, climactic action—her lie to Big Daddy about her pregnancy—is one that demands outside corroboration from Brick. Survival becomes a matter not of adhering to personal vision as it is frozen in memory, but of allowing it to interact with the present and adjust to its demands.

In *Suddenly Last Summer* Williams once again uses the monologue to examine individual versions of the past. This time, however, the essential conflict of the play is not between one character's memories and his or her present, but among several characters who attempt to control the present by establishing a causal past that suits them. To explore this contrast structurally, Williams follows O'Neill by replacing conventional dramatic climax with an expository monologue.

The central conflict of *Suddenly Last Summer* arises between two irreconcilably different remembered truths: the memories of Sebastian Venable cherished by his mother, Violet, and the very different ones held by his cousin Catharine Holly, the only witness to his awful death. To Violet, Sebastian was a sensitive and gifted poet, whose world revolved around his affection for his mother; to Catharine, he was a kindly but desperate degenerate who used both Violet and herself as unwitting procuresses of "appetizing" boys. Preserving the sanctity of her memory of Sebastian is of the utmost importance to Violet; since she has defined her own existence as the inspiration for Sebastian's poetry, both her inner reality and her outward function depend on the validity of her memories. Catharine has an opposite problem: the memory of Sebastian's hideous murder by a mob of cannibalistic children haunts her terribly, and only an injection of truth serum can force her to retell it. The major problems the play explores, then, are the nature and uses of memory, as Violet attempts to validate her remembered truths about Sebastian while Catharine seeks to escape her own very different ones. The conflict is thus not only a matter of adjusting past visions to present realities, but of determining whose vision of the past will control present and future action.

The unique structure of the play with its delayed exposition resembles the memory form of *The Glass Menagerie* in that both reflect the potency of the characters' memories and show that remembering can dominate other forms of action. As the truth serum takes its effect on Catharine and she begins to recount her tortured recollections of Sebastian's death, the squabbling of the other characters ceases, and Catharine's monologue becomes the sole activity of the play. Her halting and tormented recitation of the events she tries so hard to forget is pure exposition, transmuted from a first-act informative device to the climax of the play. All action, all conflict, and all dialogue ceases except for Catharine's verbalized memories of "the absolutely true story. No lies, nothing not spoken" (3:402). The traditional temporal sequence of a realistic, causal plot is thus disrupted by this final, retrospective monologue, and exploring the past thus assumes both thematic and structural primacy.

Because exposition of the past is displaced to the end of the play, *Suddenly Last Summer,* like O'Neill's *Long Day's Journey,* cannot reach a conventional conclusion. The imagery, actions, and dialogue of the play have all anticipated Catharine's climactic narration, and the play ends by asserting the importance of exploring alternative versions of the past rather than by choosing the validity of one over the other. Catharine's story is probably the factual truth; as Dr. Cukrowitz points out, Catharine has nothing to gain from such a grotesque fabrication. But his concluding line thrusts all such evaluation of the past into some future time not depicted in the play. *"Reflectively,"* according to the stage direction, *"into space,"* he says, "I think we ought at least to consider the possibility that the girl's story could be true . . ." (3:423). None of the issues of the play are resolved at its end: we don't know if George secures his inheritance, if the Doctor is granted his research bequest, or if Catharine will be forced to undergo the prefrontal lobotomy with which Violet hopes to erase the girl's memories. The play's refusal to reach a conclusion about the actual facts of past events or to predict future ones thrusts both past and present into the realm of limitless possibility, accessible only through the distorted filter of memory and bound together only by the fleeting present.

The Railroad Tracks and the Haunted Woodland: *A Streetcar Named Desire*

In *Vieux Carré*, *The Glass Menagerie*, and *Suddenly Last Summer*, remembered time is portrayed as the most influential component of present reality: Tom, the Writer, and Catharine all have limited ability to act in the present because they are dominated by their memories of the past. This past, however, is of a particular kind: although it has the power to prohibit other forms of action, is not a given, agreed-upon past; it is one that achieves its dominance because the characters allow it to and because the playwright has devised the structural techniques to embody it on the stage. Williams also occasionally moved beyond simply depicting an overwhelming past and created structural methods to portray the relationship between past and present—between remembered time and progressing time—as a matter of interaction, balance, and potential conflict. One such play is *A Streetcar Named Desire*.

The conflict in *Streetcar* is a double one: there is a conflict between the characters' idiosyncratic memories and what time has made of those memories, and there is a conflict between two characters who struggle to validate their incompatible visions of the past by controlling the way these visions are incorporated into the present. Stanley, "the gaudy seed-bearer" (1:256), both personifies and controls the external world of present temporal sequence, realistically portrayed; conversely, the mothlike Blanche flits and flutters through an inner world of emotional truths and memories she alone inhabits, but which Williams's antimimetic devices bring to life. The clash between the actual present and the remembered past, however, exists both within and between these two central characters.

The setting of the play is Stanley's world, bounded by the L & N railroad tracks and the streetcar line, both images of forward but constrained and predictable movement. In this world time passes conventionally, marked by the advancing stages of Stella's pregnancy and by the changing seasons. It is appropriate that the cause-and-effect sequences of the play's plot unfold according to the past information Stanley acquires about Blanche and the repercussions of his use of it. Stanley, however, is not immune to the lure of memory, and much of his present action is directed toward preserving an ideal selected moment enshrined in his memory. He tells Stella:

It's gonna be all right again between you and me the way it was. You remember the way that it was? Them nights we had together? God, honey, it's gonna be sweet when we can make noise in the night the way we used to and get the colored lights going with nobody's sister behind the curtains to hear us! (1:373)

Although Stanley continually attempts to control the present with his purposeful, one-track actions, much of his motivation for doing so stems from his desire to recapture a moment from memory that Blanche's presence denies him.

Into Stanley's sensual and directed world enters the fragile Blanche, to whom the L & N tracks seem like "the ghoul-haunted woodland of Weir" (1:252). For the aging Blanche, who craves the protection of a modern cavalier she must first attract, delaying the rushing onslaught of time is of primary importance, and many of the play's lyrical images (the soft lighting, the steamy baths) reflect her struggle to avoid the inevitable consequences of time's passage. Blanche's need to preserve the attractive appearance of youth as she remembers it, however, is accompanied by her incompatible need to escape certain memories of her own rather sordid past, and this tension within her own uses of memory leaves her an easy prey for Stanley.

Blanche and Stanley's conflict of visions is reflected structurally in the play's eloquent combination of realistic plot development and antimimetic devices. The action begins in Stanley's world, crowded noisily with a bowling alley, a sensual wife, poker buddies, a good joke. Blanche enters as an interloper into the world Stanley has constructed, a misfit in the reality he controls. Beginning with her monologue about her dead husband in scene 6, however, the staging begins to depict Blanche's unique, tormented vision as well.[6] The "hectic breakdown" of the piano music from a neighborhood saloon gives way to the haunting strains of the "Varsouviana," a "rapid, feverish" tune that the stage directions tell us is "in her mind" (1:379), but that we as auditors nevertheless hear too. The Mexican woman selling "flores para los muertos" chants in counterpoint to the accusing Mitch, with whom Stanley has shared his information about Blanche's promiscuous past. As the staging thus comes to reflect Blanche's inner perceptions, it demonstrates that her memories and fears are just as potent and just as real as the external, sequential reality in which Stanley thrives, an equally influential ingredient of their mutual present.

By the time of the climactic scene 10—Stanley's rape of Blanche— Blanche's point of view, represented expressionistically, finally becomes dominant and replaces Stanley's carefully constructed world even for the audience. As her fear of Stanley increases and she retreats further and further from the unhappy present, the landscape of Blanche's mind replaces the Kowalski apartment as the actual setting of the play. This inner landscape, however, proves just as threatening as the present moment she is trying to escape. Through the suddenly transparent back walls we see a prostitute robbing a drunkard, symbols of Blanche's sordid past and her fear of present violence. The side walls become covered with "lurid reflections [that] move sinuously as flames" (1:399), the shapes of Blanche's former passions and present terrors. The music from the nearby piano bar increases, only to be drowned out by the sound of a passing train—a sound that represents both Stanley's forward-moving world and the feared sexual attack now uppermost in Blanche's mind, and which emblematically links one with the other.

To Stanley, though, it seems as if Blanche has courted their encounter from the first, by spraying him with perfume, undressing in open doorways, and constantly demeaning him in front of his wife. Having uncovered Blanche's long history of promiscuity, Stanley sees his attack on her as part of an inevitable chain of events, the result of her past behavior both in his home and before she arrived to disrupt it. "We've had this date with each other from the beginning!" (1 : 402) he tells her. The rape scene depicts the ultimate and inevitable collision between Stanley's attempt to restore a remembered reality and Blanche's attempt to flee one and restore another, as each character inhibits the other's attempts to define a past that will partially reconstruct the disappointing present.

The passing of time in the play, however, thwarts Stanley's attempts to recapture the past as surely as Stanley himself puts an end to Blanche's flight from hers. Given Blanche's "story" about Stanley's attack on her (which Stella chooses not to believe, but with obvious reservations), and given the birth of the Kowalskis' baby (a new intruder), one doubts that things will ever be quite the same between Stella and Stanley again. And the promiscuity that Blanche has attempted to forget now becomes, in one sense, an inescapable part of her present reality, as she is forced to depend permanently on the kindness of strangers. Like *The Glass Menagerie*, this play portrays the power of memory to predominate temporarily over present reality; like *Suddenly Last Summer*, it depicts the conflicts that invariably ensue when controlling the past becomes a way to control the present and direct the future. In *A Streetcar Named Desire*, however, the balance between the power of memory and the forward thrust of time is carefully maintained and so implies (as the memory play and the retrospective monologue cannot) that neither can exist entirely independent of the other, and that character conflict is likely to focus on the conflict between selected and selective memories.

The Arrested Time of a Play-within-a-Play

In an essay entitled "The Timeless World of a Play," Williams describes the theatre's ability to dignify events and emotions that may seem inconsequential when they happen offstage, within the world of time's passing. He says:

In a play, time is arrested in the sense of being confined. By a sort of legerdemain, events are made to remain *events*, rather than being reduced so quickly to mere *occurrences*. The audience can sit back in the comforting dusk to watch a world which is flooded with light and in which emotion and action have a dimension and dignity that they would likewise have in real existence, if only the shattering intrusion of time could be locked out. (2:261–62)

Although this essay was written as a preface to *The Rose Tattoo* (1956), it also describes a more interestingly structured later work, *The Two-Character Play*.[7] In *The Two-Character Play* Williams completed the shift of emphasis begun in *Streetcar:* instead of contrasting the characters' memories and emotions with the external world of temporal sequences, each component is presented as fundamental to the characters' total reality. This present reality, however, is explicable only in terms of their continually influential, partially unfixed and unfixable past. Using the device of a play-within-a-play (unique in Williams's canon, although it is the logical extension of the memory framework in *The Glass Menagerie*), Williams demonstrates that the present can often be explained only in terms of the past, but that this past may be accessible only through present action.

The setting of *The Two-Character Play* is a divided stage, part of which represents the conventional drawing-room set of the play-within-a-play, while the other, surrounding part represents the backstage area. The two characters, Felice and Clare, are a brother-and-sister acting team at the end of their finances and at the brink of emotional collapse. The play that they perform on the inner stage is Felice's work, also entitled "The Two-Character Play," about a brother, Felice, and a sister, Clare, who are struggling to maintain their sanity after the grisly murder-suicide of their parents. The area of overlap between the interior play and the framing play is obviously quite large, and although we never know for certain how much of Felice's play is derived from his and Clare's actual past, it is clear that both players feel able to investigate the emotional reality of their present conditions only within the context of Felice's retrospective play—a memory play that differs significantly from Tom Wingfield's in that the memories are jointly maintained and are controlled in an artistic frame. Within the world of their play, the unbalanced mental states of Felice and Clare appear to be the direct result of a shattering event—their parents' deaths—and their excessive emotional tension is thereby afforded a causal logic and a dignity that they are denied in the backstage world where time has passed and adjustments must be made.

The setting of the backstage area depicts Felice and Clare's present reality. It is a freezing, shadowy, unlit room, "deepening almost to blackness at its upstage limits" (5:308), cluttered with unassembled pieces of scenery. Even though most of the action takes place on the inner stage of Felice's play, Williams claims that this backstage set is the more important of the two. In the stage directions he tells us:

> It must not only suggest the disordered images of a mind approaching collapse but also, correspondingly, the phantasmagoria of the nightmarish world that all of us live in at present, not just the subjective but the true world with all its dismaying shapes and shadows. (5:308)

The present reality of Felice and Clare is indeed nightmarish, both in the interior realm of their memories and imbalances and in the external world of their straitened circumstances. They have been deserted in a strange place by their touring company, who questioned their sanity; they have no money, no accommodations, and no means of performing a play other than their own "Two-Character Play." Felice is struggling with a recurring fear of being confined, and Clare, befuddled by liquor, exhaustion, and pills, has lost track entirely of time's passing. The usual Williams conflict between the characters' inner realities and the external, temporal world has here been collapsed into a fragmented, hallucinatory whole, and the only escape Felice and Clare can have from their terrifying present, both inner and outer, is in the more conventionally ordered world of their memory play.

In contrast to the unheated, unlit backstage area, the inner setting of their play is "filled with the benign light of a late summer afternoon" in the deep South (5:308), for the world depicted in the play-within-a-play is a version of their past, a world where the sun is warm and the terrors at least are familiar ones. The conventional fourth-wall set of a Victorian drawing room represents their ancestral home. Within its confines, Felice and Clare are able to control the shifting boundary lines between past and present, between inner and outer reality. They become, as they themselves say, "lost" in the play, immersed in an artistic rendering of their own past and engrossed in the arrested time of their play, where things can continue relatively unchanged. Within the world of their own play, Felice and Clare can control what the past has comprised and how it has affected the present; by losing themselves in the play, they find that they can enjoy the illusion of controlling time.

Near the end of their performance, however, Felice and Clare discover that their audience has walked out, and that they have been locked inside the freezing, unlit playhouse. Once again they retreat to the world of their play, where their confinement is one they have chosen, and where the rate of time's passing is seemingly subject to their control. At this point we learn that Felice's "The Two-Character Play" has not been completely written, that the players are acting from an unfinished script. Clare queries, "Do we stop where we stopped tonight or do we look for an ending?" (5:367). In one way, this failure to end the play helps the players resist the time that passes beyond their control: by leaving open a wide range of possibilities, they can avoid the inevitable results of time and the dominance of a given past and thus avert unwanted change and possible disaster. But in another, paradoxical way, not ending the play leaves Felice and Clare even more susceptible to the problems of temporality. They can avoid acknowledging the changes that external time brings, but they also lock themselves within another component of time: the specific moment that they attempt to preserve in the remembered past of their play. That they have, in fact, failed to notice the effects of time's passing on themselves is suggested by the stage directions' description of them as having "a quality of youth without being young" (5:309); that they will continue to resist time's passing is apparent from the ending of Williams's framing play, in which nothing is resolved. Felice and Clare seem doomed to exist forever in the temporarily comforting world of their play, where their attempts to lock out time make them victims of it.

By the end of *The Two-Character Play* it becomes almost impossible to distinguish the backstage Felice and Clare from their onstage avatars, or to tell how much of their play actually portrays their reality and how much of their reality invades their play. Even Clare has trouble sorting out the onstage world from the offstage one, and she accuses Felice the playwright of deliberately obscuring the dividing line. She says, "Sometimes you work on a play by inventing situations in life that, that—correspond to those in the play, and you're so skillful at it that even I'm taken in" (5:365). Williams's overlapping of these two separate realities is, of course, one point of the play: what is real and true at one moment and in one context may not be so in another. In "The Timeless World of a Play" Williams remarks:

> Truth is fragmentary at best: we love and betray each other not quite in the same breath but in two breaths that occur in fairly close sequence. But the

fact that passion occurred in *passing* . . . should not be regarded as proof of its inconsequence. And this is the very truth that drama wishes to bring us. (2:261)

The "truth" of Felice and Clare's world is fragmentary to the point of being bizarre, but the continuing truth of their condition—their loneliness, their despair, their love for and dependence on each other—is the most important truth, one made apparent structurally by the device of a play-within-a-play.

The Fragmentary Truth

In an early one-act memory play entitled *The Long Goodbye*, a character named Joe, while watching furniture movers empty his apartment, complains that his life is nothing but "a long, long goodbye!"[8] As early as 1953, then, when this work was published in *27 Wagon Loads of Cotton*, Williams was concerned with his characters' responses to their pasts and was already using "plastic" theatrical devices (such as the dead mother and sister that Joe remembers, walking undisturbed among the moving men) to depict the vitality of memory. Throughout his career this theme is repeated: he continually asserts, through a variety of dramatic devices (from memory frameworks to monologues to a play-within-a-play), that memory is the most important constructor of past truths, even when it is at odds with what the past has become in the present. His characters continually shore up the fragments of their pasts as protection against the onslaught of time, but fragments—partial truths—they remain.

Because the remembered truth is only a part of present reality, Williams's plays also consistently depict the passage of time, which often contradicts memory and forces it to change. This alternation of memory and passing time, represented structurally by alternating antimimetic and realistic techniques, evidently produces much of the dramatic intensity of Williams's best plays, for his weakest efforts are those that omit one component or the other. Witness *In the Bar of a Tokyo Hotel*, in which the narrated memories remain unconvincing, unlike the vividly embodied and compelling memories of Tom Wingfield or Blanche Dubois. Witness also *I Rise in Flame, Cried the Phoenix*, in which time seems not to pass at all, and the dramatic conflict between memory and the present is lost.

Many of Williams's other plays also succeed at dramatizing the conflict between remembered time and progressing time. One thinks immediately of *Camino Real*, which succeeds through symbolic density rather than through alternation of antimimetic and realistic techniques, or *The Night of the Iguana*, where the conflict between "the realistic level and the fantastic level" of life (as Shannon describes it—4:317) is internalized within the characters and leads them, with Hannah Jelkes's help, to accept both levels as "real." For Williams's characters are perpetually confronted with a double vision of time: they understand and acknowledge the power of the past they remember, but they too often fail to incorporate this remembered past into the present time that proceeds apace around them. Very few of them ever share Hannah Jelkes's awareness that both versions of time—that of memory's arrested vision and that of the sequence of passing moments—are equally real, equally valid, and equally important components of present reality, or that each vision by itself is "fragmentary, at best." This is the stereoscopic vision of time characteristic of Williams's best work, a vision not usually accessible to the naked eye, but embodied on the stage and made manifest to the audience by Williams's ever-changing, ever-innovative combination of antimimetic devices within the larger framework of the formally realistic play.

Conclusion

The Presence of the Past

> Time past and time future
> What might have been and what has been
> Point to one end, which is always present.
> —T. S. Eliot, "Burnt Norton"

The past is an inescapable part of the present in modern American drama. As demonstrated in the plays of the four writers discussed in this work—O'Neill, Wilder, Miller, and Williams—the past no longer consists solely of verifiable anterior action. Rather, the past in these plays becomes a matter of inquiry and debate; it directs characters' choices, becomes a source of their conflicts, remains alive in their memories, and even changes through time. In these plays, the past repeatedly interacts with the present in complex and often surprising ways.

This vision of the past as both persistent and debatable was not readily available to playwrights at the beginning of the twentieth century. Both O'Neill and Wilder remembered the theatre of their youth as a forum for well-made plays and melodramas. It was a rigidly conventional world in which the stage past comprised a series of specific, causal incidents that could be revealed by any "not too improbable" mechanical device. Once these twentieth-century playwrights recongnized the past as not merely factual, not necessarily causal, and never wholly separable from the present, they refined dramatic form to accommodate it. Their interest in an ever-present past became a thematic imperative for structural change.

Eugene O'Neill began these reforms by experimenting with exposition, the element of dramatic structure that has traditionally defined the relationship of past to present. For O'Neill, the past included not only the causal incidents of formal realism, but also the shifting, individual memories of his characters. O'Neill therefore reclaimed a number of antimimetic expository devices—asides, soliloquies, masks—to incorporate this unverifiable, idiosyncratic past into the realistic framework of the stage world he was creating. Once he had expanded the influence of the past with these techniques, however, O'Neill took the process a step further: he reshaped the entire structure of realistic drama, allowing exposition to subsume conventional conflict and making resolution nearly impossible. In this new, expository version of realistic drama, the past is not prior to the present but central to it.

Like O'Neill, Thornton Wilder envisioned the past as more than a sequence of preceding events. For Wilder, however, the dramatic problem was how to portray "two times at once": the "present" as characters perceive it, and the "past" as history records it. To examine the role of the moment in shaping the patterns of history, Wilder developed a number of innovative techniques: an unlocalized stage; intermingled historical eras; the achronological handling of stage time; an obtrusive Stage Manager, who offers multiple perspectives on passing moments. Despite Wilder's modesty about his place in dramatic history, his "rediscovery of forgotten goods" expanded the temporal boundaries of the modern American stage and allowed his successors to connect the past to the present in multiple ways.

Throughout his career Arthur Miller has been concerned with the relationship between actions and their consequences—yet another version of the relationship between past and present. Early in his careeer, portraying this past simply entailed revealing a specific secret through a realistic chain of events. As his concept of the past's involvement with the present evolved, however, Miller's dramatic forms became more innovative. Like O'Neill, he began his experiments with antimimetic devices designed to reveal the past's lingering influence; imaginary leaves, remembered music, and embodied memories all invade the present of Miller's plays. His mature works, however, like O'Neill's, depend less upon experimental devices and more upon a restructured, exploratory dramatic form. In Miller's major plays since the late 1960s, the past is not a secret to be disclosed but a web of possibilities to be investigated; causal actions are not merely hidden from the audience but are unrecognized by the characters who grope through their memories to locate them. In this way Miller has extended the expository dramas of O'Neill, since now the characters themselves are unsure of what is to be "exposed" or how it has contributed to the present.

For Tennessee Williams, the remembered past retains immense power in the present. One of Williams's recurring concerns, therefore, was to depict on the stage the vitality of memory. Devices like the memory framework, slide projections, and monologues attest to the success of his endeavor. Despite the importance of memories to his characters, however, time continues to pass around them; Williams, like Wilder, was interested in portraying "two times at once." In order to depict this recurring conflict between time passing and time suspended, between clock time and interior time, Williams characteristically constructed plots with the linear causality of formal realism, even while his characters inhabit a world of shadow images, remembered music, dissolving walls, and haunted rooms. This combination of formal realism with "plastic" theatrical devices enabled Williams to demonstrate the immediacy of the past as well as its inevitable collision with the present.

As a result of these four playwrights' shared interest in the presence of the past, American dramatic form has changed profoundly over the course of the twentieth century. The otherwise formally realistic American stage is now capable of relating past to present in multiple ways and of portraying time both as characters remember it and as it passes around them. In the modern American stage world, the past is never radically separate from the present.

Of course, modern American playwrights are not unique in attempting to relate past to present in innovative ways. As I described in chapter 1, the playwrights of each era in dramatic history had a distinctive idea of what the past is and developed traditions for presenting it on the stage. But while modern American techniques for mingling past and present are not without precedent, neither are they mere imitations of existing models. American playwrights of the twentieth century have developed a new tradition as a result of their experiments, a tradition with two defining elements: a belief that the past does not simply precede the present but forms a crucial part of it; and an adherence, for the most part, to the techniques of formal realism, with deviations typically emerging to include the past in the present.

In thus reshaping the modern realistic idiom, the four dramatists studied here have offered their successors alternative possibilities for creating appropriate dramatic action. The once separate components of formal realism—exposition, complication, climax, and denoue-ment—are no longer clearly separable. One might say that the single line of a formally realistic plot has been looped over itself to form a spiral: the characters' tracing and retracing of what they have been in the past affords them greater self-knowledge, greater understanding of the present, and it sometimes replaces more conventional dramatic "action."

As S. H. Butcher cautioned almost a century ago, this "retrograde" movement inhibits dramatic progress of the usual sort. Yet it is pre-cisely this retrospective aspect of American dramatic form that has had the most widely influential repercusssions. In the stage world that twenty-first-century playwrights will soon inherit, the past has be-come an integral part of what once seemed an independent present.

Notes

Chapter 1. An Endless Retrograde Movement

1. Thornton Wilder, "Preface," in *Three Plays* (New York: Harper, 1957), xi.

2. Peter Szondi, quoted and translated in Keir Elam, *The Semiotics of Theatre and Drama* (London: Methuen, 1980), 115.

3. Elam, *Semiotics of Theatre*, 117–18.

4. Thomas S. Kuhn, in *The Structure of Scientific Revolutions*, explains that the rejection of one time-honored theory in favor of a new, incompatible theory causes a shift not only in the accepted mode of inquiry but also in the nature of the problems available for scrutiny (2d ed. [Chicago: University of Chicago Press, 1970], 6). A close look at the changing conventions of dramatic structure will reveal a similar "paradigm shift": as each playwright devises new techniques to relate past to present, he or she opens new temporal relationships to portray new possible links between past and present.

5. V. A. Kolve, *The Play Called Corpus Christi* (Stanford, Calif.: Stanford University Press, 1966), 48–63.

6. Alan S. Downer, *The British Drama: A Brief Handbook and Chronicle* (New York: Appleton-Century-Crofts, 1950), 16.

7. Stephen S. Stanton, "Introduction," in *Camille and Other Plays* (New York: Hill and Wang, 1957), xiv.

8. George Bernard Shaw, *Shaw's Dramatic Criticism*, ed. John F. Matthews (New York: Hill and Wang, 1959), 22.

9. William Archer, *Play-making: A Manual of Craftsmanship* (1912; reprint, New York: Dover, 1960), 77.

10. George Pierce Baker, *Dramatic Technique* (Boston: Houghton Mifflin, 1919), 167–71.

11. Ibid., 167.

12. Ibid., 172.

13. S. H. Butcher, *Aristotle's Theory of Poetry and Fine Art* (1894; reprint, New York: Dover, 1951).

14. Among the many critics who have defined American literature as a product of

recurring contrasts or discussed the complex American attitudes toward the past are Richard Chase, *The American Novel and Its Tradition* (Garden City, N.Y.: Doubleday, 1957); Henry Steele Commager, *The Search for a Usable Past* (New York: Knopf, 1967); Joseph G. Kronick, *American Poetics of History* (Baton Rouge: Louisiana State University Press, 1984); R. W. B. Lewis, *The American Adam* (Chicago: University of Chicago Press, 1955); Perry Miller, introduction to Benjamin Franklin and Jonathan Edwards, in *Major Writers of America*, ed. Perry Miller (New York: Harcourt, 1962), 83–97; Richard Poirier, *A World Elsewhere* (London: Oxford University Press, 1966); and Thomas Daniel Young, *The Past in the Present: A Thematic Study of Modern Southern Fiction* (Baton Rouge: Lousiana State University Press, 1981).

15. Cleanth Brooks, R. W. B. Lewis, and Robert Penn Warren, *American Literature: The Makers and the Making* (New York: St. Martin's, 1973), 1 : 15.

16. Although I emphasize the Puritan historians because their sense of a religious mission added a certain zeal to their records, it is clear that the early settlers of many colonies were aware of themselves as actors in a unique historical drama. The founding of a new world, after all, was bound to be of immense historical significance. This sense of the importance of their lives for future generations is borne out by the frequent use of the word "history" in the titles of their written works: we have John Smith's *The Generall Historie of Virginia* (1624), John Winthrop's *The History of New England* (1826), and William Byrd's *History of the Dividing Line* (1728; pub. 1841), to name only an obvious few. Clearly, these early colonists were consciously escaping history while troubling to establish their own places in it.

17. Lewis, *American Adam*, 197.

18. Crèvecoeur, Hector St. John, *Letters from an American Farmer* (1782; reprint, London: J. M. Dent, 1951), 43–44.

19. Quoted in Lewis, *American Adam*, 5.

20. Commager, *Search for a Usable Past*, 25–27.

21. Ralph Waldo Emerson, *Complete Writings* (New York: Wise, 1929), 1 : 1.

22. Charles Beard, "Written History As an Act of Faith" (1933), in *Readings in Society and Thought in America*, ed. Harvey Wish (New York: McKay, 1970), 272.

23. Ibsen's method has been called "retrospective" for so long that critics no longer bother to document their sources for this description. As early as 1922 Thomas Moody Campbell uses the term "retrospective analysis" and in 1931 Harley Granville-Barker explains it fully. See Campbell, *Hebbel, Ibsen, and the Retrospective Analysis* (Heidelberg: C. Winter, 1922), Granville-Barker, *On Dramatic Method* (London: Sidgwick and Jackson, 1931), 177–78.

24. See Louis Broussard, *American Drama: Contemporary Allegory From Eugene O'Neill to Tennessee Williams* (Norman: University of Oklahoma Press, 1962), and Alan S. Downer, *Fifty Years of American Drama: 1900–1950* (Chicago: Henry Regnery, 1951), 93.

25. For a concise introduction to the philosophical backgrounds of expressionism see R. S. Furness, *Expressionism* (London: Methuen, 1973); for a more extensive analysis see Walter Sokel, *The Writer in Extremis* (Stanford, Calif.: Stanford University Press, 1959). For an examination of the dramatic devices of expressionism and the influence of expressionism on American drama see Peter Bauland, *The Hooded Eagle* (Syracuse, N.Y.: Syracuse University Press, 1968); Oscar G. Brockett, *Perspectives on Contemporary Theatre* (Baton Rouge: Louisiana State University Press, 1971); Broussard, *American Drama;* Downer, *Fifty Years;* John Gassner, *Form and Idea in Modern Theatre* (New York: Dryden, 1956) and *Theatre at the Crossroads: Plays and Playwrights of the Mid-Century American Stage* (New York: Holt, Rinehart, and Winston, 1960); and Mardi Valgemae, *Accelerated Grimace: Expressionism in the American Drama of the 1920s* (Carbondale: Southern Illinois University Press, 1972).

Chapter 2. Eugene O'Neill: What the Past Has Made Them

1. Eugene O'Neill, quoted in *O'Neill and His Plays: Four Decades of Criticism*, ed. Oscar Cargill et al. (New York: New York University Press, 1961), 111.

2. O'Neill, *Long Day's Journey into Night* (New Haven: Yale University Press, 1956), 64. Hereafter cited by page number in the text.

3. For some helpful strategies for dividing O'Neill's career into discrete stages, see Francis Fergusson, "Melodramatist," in Cargill, *O'Neill and His Plays*, 271–82; Hylbert Norman Opper, "Exposition in the Plays of Eugene O'Neill" (M.A. thesis, Northwestern University, 1937); John Henry Raleigh, *The Plays of Eugene O'Neill* (Carbondale: Southern Illinois University Press, 1965), 195; Rudolf Stamm, "The Dramatic Experiments of Eugene O'Neill," *English Studies* 28 (1947): 1–15; Robert F. Whitman, "O'Neill's Search for a 'Language of the Theatre,'" in *O'Neill: A Collection of Critical Essays*, ed. John Gassner (Englewood Cliffs, N.J.: Prentice-Hall, 1964), 142–64.

4. Michael Selmon, "Past, Present, and Future Converged: The Place of *More Stately Mansions* in the Eugene O'Neill Canon," *Modern Drama* 28 (1985): 556–57.

5. Eugene M. Waith, "Eugene O'Neill: An Exercise in Unmasking," *Educational Theatre Journal* 13 (1960): 182–91.

6. O'Neill, *The Moon of the Caribbees*, in *The Plays of Eugene O'Neill* (New York: Random House, 1955), 1:456. The plays collected in this edition will hereafter be cited in the text by volume and page number.

7. Quoted in Arthur Gelb and Barbara Gelb, *O'Neill* (New York: Harper and Row, 1962), 701.

8. Quoted in Barrett H. Clark, *Eugene O'Neill: The Man and His Plays* (New York: Dover, 1947), 60.

9. Quoted in Paul Voelker, "Eugene O'Neill's Aesthetic of the Drama," *Modern Drama* 21 (1978): 91–92.

10. William Jennings Adams, "The Dramatic Structure of the Plays of Eugene O'Neill" (Ph.D. diss., Stanford University, 1956), 155.

11. Raleigh, *Plays*, 177–79.

12. Heywood Broun, review of *Gold*, by Eugene O'Neill, in Cargill, *O'Neill and His Plays*, 150–51.

13. O'Neill, "Memoranda on Masks," *American Spectator*, November 1932, 3.

14. O'Neill, quoted in Gelb and Gelb, *O'Neill*, 628.

15. John Howard Lawson, "Eugene O'Neill," in Gassner, *O'Neill*, 47.

16. For an interesting analysis of the structural similarities between *The Emperor Jones* and the late plays, see Lisa M. Schwerdt, "Blueprint for the Future: *The Emperor Jones*," in *Critical Essays on Eugene O'Neill*, ed. James J. Martine (Boston: G.K. Hall, 1984), 72–75.

17. Some audiences have been bothered by the apparent racism of *The Emperor Jones*, feeling that O'Neill has depicted Jones's racial past as insultingly primitive. Although O'Neill's concept of a racial past is, of course, reductive, I do not agree that bigotry is necessarily the source of the problem. *The Hairy Ape*, written during the same era, places a white man, Yank, in a similar situation, and ends by asserting how little humankind has evolved from the apes. Apparently O'Neill was simply trying to demonstrate the hidden, primal urges that he felt we all share, and to embody them on the stage.

18. Eric Bentley, "Trying to Like O'Neill," *Kenyon Review* 14 (1952): 483. O'Neill is quoted in Gelb and Gelb, *O'Neill*, as having said that he "got terribly messed up in searching for new ways and means and styles" (722).

19. O'Neill, quoted in *American Playwrights on Drama*, ed. Horst Frenz (New York: Hill and Wang, 1965), 11.
20. O'Neill, quoted in Gelb and Gelb, *O'Neill*, 722–23.
21. Stark Young, "Eugene O'Neill's New Play," in Gassner, *O'Neill*, 82–88.
22. Waith, "Eugene O'Neill," 34; Rudolf Stamm, "'Faithful Realism': Eugene O'Neill and the Problem of Style," *English Studies* 40 (1959): 245–48; Raleigh, *Plays*, 195.
23. O'Neill, *A Touch of the Poet* (New Haven: Yale University Press, 1957), 63.
24. Hewes, quoted in Cargill, *O'Neill and His Plays*, 223.
25. My discussion of the similarities among the three late plays is informed throughout by John Henry Raleigh's analysis of the formal properties of *Iceman* in his "Introduction" to *Twentieth Century Interpretations of "The Iceman Cometh"* (Englewood Cliffs, N.J.: Prentice-Hall, 1968), 9–12.
26. Raleigh, *Twentieth Century Interpretations*, 9; Whitman, "O'Neill's Search," 160–64; Brenda Murphy, "O'Neill's Realism: A Structural Approach," *Eugene O'Neill Newsletter* 7, no. 2 (Summer/Fall 1983): 4.
27. Tom Driver, "On the Late Plays of Eugene O'Neill," in Gassner, *O'Neill*, 113.
28. O'Neill, quoted in James Milton Highsmith, "The Cornell Letters: Eugene O'Neill on his Craftsmanship to George Jean Nathan," *Modern Drama* 15, no. 1 (1972): 86.
29. O'Neill, quoted in Gelb and Gelb, *O'Neill*, 481.

Chapter 3. Thornton Wilder: Disparate Moments and Repetitive Patterns

1. Malcolm Cowley, "The Man Who Abolished Time," *Saturday Review* 6 (October 1956): 51.
2. Cowley, *A Second Flowering: Works and Days of the Lost Generation* (New York: Viking, 1973), 126–27.
3. Thornton Wilder, "Preface," in *Three Plays*, x–xi.
4. Ibid., xiii.
5. Wilder, "Forward," in *The Angel That Troubled the Waters, and Other Plays* (New York: Coward-McCann, 1928), xiii. References to this volume will hereafter be cited by page number in the text.
6. Malcolm Goldstein, *The Art of Thornton Wilder* (Lincoln: University of Nebraska Press, 1965), 31.
7. Wilder, "Preface," in *Three Plays*, x–xi.
8. Wilder, "Some Thoughts on Playwriting," in Frenz, *American Playwrights*, 59.
9. William A. Scally, "Modern Return to Medieval Drama," in *The Many Forms of Drama*, ed. Karelisa V. Hartigan (Lanham, Md.: University Press of America, 1985), 107.
10. Wilder, "Thoughts on Playwriting," 60.
11. In "The Dramatic Techniques of Thornton Wilder and Bertolt Brecht: A Study in Comparison," *Modern Drama* 15 (1972): 112–24, Douglas Charles Wixon, Jr., explores in detail the similarities between the two playwrights' dramatic structures, emphasizing their mutual use of overt theatricalism, minimal characterization, symbolic rather than naturalistic staging, and episodic structure. Although Wixon hesitates to assign any direct influence from Brecht to Wilder, he argues convincingly

for Wilder's familiarity with Brecht's work after the former's 1928 lecture trip to Germany.

See also Francis Fergusson, "Three Allegorists: Brecht, Wilder, and Eliot," *Sewanee Review* 64 (Autumn 1956): 544–73. Fergusson stresses not so much the similarity of technique, but similarity of didactic intent between Wilder and Brecht.

12. Wilder, "Preface," in *Three Plays*, xiv.

13. Wilder, "Preface" to *Our Town*, in *American Characteristics and Other Essays*, ed. Donald Gallup (New York: Harper and Row, 1979), 101.

14. Wilder, *The Long Christmas Dinner and Other Plays in One Act* (New York: Coward-McCann; New Haven: Yale University Press, 1931), 19, 23. Plays in this volume will hereafter be cited by page number in the text.

15. Wilder, "Preface" to *Our Town*, 102.

16. Wilder, *Our Town*, in *Three Plays*, 9. Hereafter cited by page number in the text.

17. For a different interpretation of the role of memory in *Our Town* see Donald Haberman, *The Plays of Thornton Wilder* (Middletown, Conn.: Wesleyan University Press, 1967), 57–59. Haberman's analysis of Wilder's "inverse flashbacks" is both interesting and illuminating, although I disagree with his conclusion that "Wilder offers memory as the real thing, feeling that it has a greater value than actual experience."

18. Wilder, "Preface" to *Our Town*, 101.

19. Wilder, *The Skin of Our Teeth*, in *Three Plays*, 110. Hereafter cited by page number in the text.

20. Wilder, quoted in Richard H. Goldstone, interview with Thornton Wilder, in *Writers at Work: The Paris Review Interviews*, ed. Malcolm Cowley (New York: Viking, 1958), 114.

Chapter 4. Arthur Miller: Illuminating Process

1. "Introduction," in *Collected Plays* (New York: Viking Press, 1981), 18.

2. Arthur Miller, quoted in Ronald Hayman, *Arthur Miller* (New York: Ungar, 1972), 15. Hayman's thesis, like my own, is that Miller's interest in process forms the matrix for his career. What Hayman does not explore, however, is Miller's changing definition of what process entails, or the different kinds of processes each play presents.

3. Miller, Arthur, "Introduction," in *Collected Plays*, 21.

4. Ibid., 23.

5. Miller, Arthur, quoted in Hayman, *Arthur Miller*, 17.

6. See, for example, C. W. E. Bigsby, *Confrontation and Commitment: A Study of Contemporary American Drama 1959–1966* (Columbia, Mo.: University of Missouri Press, 1967), 28–29; Raymond Williams, *Drama from Ibsen to Brecht* (New York: Oxford University Press, 1969), 268–69; and Tom Scanlan, *Family, Drama, and American Dreams* (Westport, Conn.: Greenwood Press, 1978), 131.

7. Miller, Arthur, "Introduction," in *Collected Plays*, 20.

8. Ibid., 18.

9. Miller, Arthur, *Collected Plays*, 1:74. Works in this collection will be cited hereafter in the text by volume and page number.

10. For representative samples of such criticism see Eric Bentley, *What is Theatre?* (New York: Atheneum, 1968), 26; John Mander, *The Writer and Commitment* (London: Secker and Warburg, 1961), 151; Edward Murray, *Arthur Miller, Dramatist* (New York: Frederick Ungar, 1967), 180; and Orm Överland, "The Action and Its Significance:

Arthur Miller's Struggle with Dramatic Form," *Modern Drama* 18 (1975): 1–14. Överland's summary of this attack on Miller's work is particularly helpful.

11. Dennis Welland, *Miller: A Study of His Plays* (London: Eyre Methuen, 1979), 40.

12. Sir Laurence Olivier, letter to Arthur Miller, in *The Crucible: Text and Criticism,* ed. Gerald Weales (New York: Viking, 1971), 153.

13. Miller, Arthur, "It Could Happen Here—And Did," in *The Theater Essays of Arthur Miller,* ed. Robert A. Martin (New York: Viking Press, 1978), 295.

14. Miller, Arthur, "Introduction," in *Collected Plays,* 41.

15. Ibid., 18.

16. See, for example, John H. Ferres, "Introduction," in *Twentieth Century Interpretations of "The Crucible,"* ed. John H. Ferres (Englewood Cliffs, N.J.: Prentice-Hall, 1972), 14.

17. Miller, Arthur, "On Social Plays," in *Theater Essays,* 63.

18. Miller, Arthur, "What Makes Plays Endure?" in *Theater Essays,* 261.

19. Miller, Arthur, "Introduction," in *Collected Plays,* 24.

20. Ibid., 23.

21. Downer has noted that the *Salesman* method was a major departure from Ibsenian realism; he says: "The effect [of Ibsen's retrospective technique] was to show simultaneously the cause and the event, so that the theme became inescapable. Miller's innovation is in the direction of more complete visualization; what Ibsen was content to leave as narrative, information conveyed by dialogue, Miller dramatizes" (*Fifty Years,* 73–74). What Downer does not mention, however, is that in *Death of a Salesman* the causes of events are not clear to the central character, and that the process of locating and confronting these causes is the central action of the play.

22. Miller, Arthur, "Introduction," in *Collected Plays,* 26.

23. Ibid., 27.

24. Miller, Arthur, "The Shadows of the Gods," in *Theater Essays,* 185.

25. See, for example, Hayman, *Arthur Miller,* 85–94; Murray, *Arthur Miller, Dramatist,* 154–55; and Welland, *Miller,* 94–98.

26. Miller, Arthur, quoted in Hayman, *Arthur Miller,* 18.

27. Miller, Arthur, "Shadows of the Gods," 189.

28. Welland, *Miller,* 139.

29. Miller, Arthur, *Danger: Memory!* (New York: Grove Press, 1986), 53. Hereafter cited by page number in the text.

Chapter 5. Tennessee Williams: Memory and the Passing Moment

1. Tennessee Williams, *The Theatre of Tennessee Williams* (New York: New Directions, 1971–76), 5:46. Unless otherwise noted, all quotations from Williams will be taken from this source and cited by volume and page number in the text.

2. Williams, *Dragon Country* (New York: New Directions, 1970), 141.

3. A number of scholars have commented on Williams's characteristic combination of realistic and antimimetic devices. See Ruby Cohn, "The Garrulous Grotesques of Tennessee Williams," in *Tennessee Williams: A Collection of Critical Essays,* ed. Stephen S. Stanton (Englewood Cliffs, N.J.: Prentice-Hall, 1977), 55–56; Mary Ann Corrigan, "Beyond Verisimilitude: Echoes of Expressionism in Williams' Plays," in *Tennessee Williams: A Tribute,* ed. Jac Tharpe (Jackson, Miss.: University Press of Mississippi, 1977), 395; Benjamin Nelson, *Tennessee Williams: The Man and His Work*

(New York: Ivan Obolensky, 1961), 180; and Gerald Weales, "Tennessee Williams' Achievement in the Sixties," in Stanton, *Tennessee Williams*, 61. These writers have not, however, explored the playwright's use of these devices in the temporal context I see as central to their function.

Conversely, others have argued that time is the principal antagonist in Williams's dramas, but they have not investigated the structural manifestations of the distinction between external time and the imposed temporality of memory. See Billy Mishoe, "Time as Antagonist in the Dramas of Tennessee Williams" (Ph.D. diss., Florida State University, 1972), and Henry Popkin, "The Plays of Tennessee Williams," *Tulane Drama Review* 4, no. 3 (March 1960): 54.

4. R. B. Parker argues convincingly for the superiority of the so-called reading edition of *The Glass Menagerie*, which retains the screen and other antimimetic devices, over the "acting edition" based on the original production. For Parker, the complex relationship between the past Tom remembers and his obsessive act of remembering it (a relationship I discuss later in this chapter) is preserved in all its ambiguity only through the antimimetic staging. See Parker, "The Circle Closed: A Psychological Reading of *The Glass Menagerie* and *The Two Character Play*," *Modern Drama* 28 1985): 517–34.

See also the illuminating discussion of Williams's devising the memory play structure in Paul T. Nolan, "Two Memory Plays: *The Glass Menagerie* and *After the Fall*," *McNeese Review* 17 (1966): 27–38.

5. Williams, *Vieux Carré* (New York: New Directions, 1979), 115.

6. Elia Kazan, the play's first director, explains that "one reason a 'style,' a stylized production is necessary is that a subjective factor—Blanche's memories, her inner life, emotions are a real factor. We cannot understand her behavior unless we see the effect of her past on her present behavior." See Kazan, "Notebook for *A Streetcar Named Desire*," in *Twentieth Century Interpretations of "A Streetcar Named Desire*," ed. Jordan Y. Miller (Englewood Cliffs, N.J.: Prentice-Hall, 1971), 21.

7. *The Two-Character Play* (sometimes entitled *Out Cry*) went through many versions and revisions between 1967 and 1975. The version published in vol. 5 of *The Theatre of Tennessee Williams* is the one I discuss here.

8. Williams, *The Long Goodbye*, in *27 Wagons Full of Cotton, and Other One-Act Plays* (1945; reprint, New York: New Directions, 1953), 178.

Select Bibliography

The bibliography includes all cited sources as well as other sources that have influenced this study and may prove useful to an interested reader.

Adams, William Jennings. "The Dramatic Structure of the Plays of Eugene O'Neill." Ph.D. diss., Stanford University, 1956.

Archer, William. *Play-making: A Manual of Craftsmanship.* 1912, Reprint. New York: Dover, 1960.

Baker, George Pierce. *Dramatic Technique.* Boston: Houghton Mifflin, 1919.

Ballet, Arthur H. "In Our Living and in Our Dying." *English Journal* 45 (1956): 243–49.

Barlow, Judith. *Final Acts: The Creation of Three Late O'Neill Plays.* Athens: The University of Georgia Press, 1985.

Bauland, Peter. *The Hooded Eagle.* Syracuse, N.Y.: Syracuse University Press, 1968.

Beard, Charles. "Written History as an Act of Faith." Presidential address delivered before the American Historical Association, 28 December 1933. In *Readings in Society and Thought in America,* edited by Harvey Wish. New York: McKay, 1970.

Bentley, Eric. *The Playwright as Thinker: A Study of Drama in Modern Times.* New York: Harcourt, Brace, and World, 1967.

———. "Trying to Like O'Neill." *Kenyon Review* 14 (1952): 476–92.

———. *What is Theatre? Incorporating the Dramatic Event and Other Reviews 1944–1967.* New York: Atheneum, 1968.

Berlin, Normand. "Complementarity in *A Streetcar Named Desire.*" In *Tennessee Williams: A Tribute,* edited by Jac Tharpe, 97–103. Jackson, Miss.: University Press of Mississippi, 1977.

Bigsby, C. W. E. *Confrontation and Commitment: A Study of Contemporary American Drama 1959–1966.* Columiba, Mo.: University of Missouri Press, 1967.

———. *A Critical Introduction to Twentieth-Century American Drama.* Volume 2. Cambridge: Cambridge University Press, 1984.

Bluefarb, Sam. "*The Glass Menagerie:* Three Visions of Time." *College English* 24 (1963): 513–18.

Bogard, Travis. *Contour in Time: The Plays of Eugene O'Neill.* New York: Oxford University Press, 1972.

Brockett, Oscar G. *Perspectives on Contemporary Theatre*. Baton Rouge: Louisiana State University Press, 1971.

Brooks, Cleanth, R. W. B. Lewis, and Robert Penn Warren. *American Literature: The Makers and the Making*. 2 vols. New York: St. Martin's, 1973.

Broun, Heywood. Review of *Gold*, by Eugene O'Neill. In *O'Neill and His Plays: Four Decades of Criticism*, edited by Oscar Cargill et al., 150–51. New York: New York University Press, 1961. (First published in *New York Tribune*, 2 June 1921.)

Broussard, Louis. *American Drama: Contemporary Allegory from Eugene O'Neill to Tennessee Williams*. Norman: University of Oklahoma Press, 1962.

Butcher, S. H. *Aristotle's Theory of Poetry and Fine Art*. 1894. Reprint. New York: Dover, 1951.

Byrd, William. *History of the Dividing Line*. In *The Prose Works of William Byrd of Westover*, edited by Louis B. Wright, 157–336. Cambridge: Harvard University Press, Belknap Press, 1966.

Campbell, Joseph, and Henry Morton Robinson. "The Skin of Whose Teeth?" *Saturday Review of Literature* 25 (19 December 1942): 3–4.

———. "The Skin of Whose Teeth? Part II: The Intention Behind the Deed." *Saturday Review of Literature* 26 (26 February 1943): 16, 18–19.

Campbell, Thomas Moody. *Hebbel, Ibsen, and the Retrospective Analysis*. Heidelberg: C. Winter, 1922.

Cargill, Oscar, et al., eds. *O'Neill and His Plays: Four Decades of Criticism*. New York: New York University Press, 1961.

Casty, Alan. "Post-Loverly Love: A Comparative Report." *Antioch Review* 26 (Fall 1966): 399–411.

Cerf, Walter. "Psychoanalysis and the Realistic Drama." *Journal of Aesthetics and Art Criticism* 16, no. 3 (1958): 328–36.

Chase, Richard. *The American Novel and Its Tradition*. Garden City, N.Y.: Doubleday, 1957.

Chothia, Jean. *Forging a Language: A Study of the Plays of Eugene O'Neill*. Cambridge: Cambridge University Press, 1979.

Clark, Barrett H. *Eugene O'Neill: The Man and His Plays*. New York: Dover, 1947.

Cohn, Ruby. "The Garrulous Grotesques of Tennessee Williams." In *Tennessee Williams: A Collection of Critical Essays*, edited by Stephen S. Stanton, 45–60. Englewood Cliffs, N.J.: Prentice-Hall, 1977.

Commager, Henry Steele. *The Search for a Usable Past*. New York: Knopf, 1967.

Corrigan, Mary Ann. "Beyond Verisimilitude: Echoes of Expressionism in Williams' Plays." In *Tennessee Williams: A Tribute*, edited by Jac Tharpe, 375–412. Jackson, Miss.: University Press of Mississippi, 1977.

———. "Memory, Dream and Myth in the Plays of Tennessee Williams." *Renascence* 28 (Spring 1976): 155–67.

Corrigan, Robert W., ed. *Arthur Miller: A Collection of Critical Essays*. Twentieth Century Views Series. Englewood Cliffs, N.J.: Prentice-Hall, 1969.

———. "Thornton Wilder and the Tragic Sense of Life." *Educational Theatre Journal* 13 (1961): 161–73.

Cowley, Malcolm. "The Man Who Abolished Time." *Saturday Review of Literature* 6 (October 1956): 13–14, 50–52.

————. *A Second Flowering: Works and Days of the Lost Generation*. New York: Viking, 1973.

Crèvecoeur, Hector St. John. *Letters from an American Farmer.* 1782. Reprint. London: J. M. Dent, 1951.

Culler, Jonathan. *Structuralist Poetics*. Ithaca: Cornell University Press, 1975.

de Man, Paul. "Literary History and Literary Modernity." In *Blindness and Insight: Essays in the Rhetoric of Contemporary Criticism*. New York: Oxford University Press, 1971.

Downer, Alan S. *The British Drama: A Brief Handbook and Chronicle*. New York: Appleton-Century-Crofts, 1950.

————. *Fifty Years of American Drama: 1900–1950*. Chicago: Henry Regnery, 1951.

————. "Old, Borrowed, and (a Trifle) Blue: Notes on the New York Theatre, 1967–68." In *Critical Essays on Arthur Miller,* edited by James J.Martine, 155–57. Boston: G. K. Hall, 1979. (First published in *Quarterly Journal of Speech* 54, [1968]: 203–6.)

————. *Recent American Drama*. University of Minnesota Pamphlets on American Writers, no. 7. Minneapolis: University of Minnesota Press, 1961.

————, ed. *The American Theater Today*. New York: Basic Books, 1967.

Driver, Tom. "On the Late Plays of Eugene O'Neill." In *O'Neill: A Collection of Critical Essays,* edited by John Gassner, 110–23. Englewood Cliffs, N.J.: Prentice-Hall, 1964.

Dusenberry, Winifred L. *The Theme of Loneliness in Modern American Drama*. Gainesville: University of Florida Press, 1960.

Elam, Keir. *The Semiotics of Theatre and Drama*. London: Methuen, 1980.

Emerson, Ralph Waldo. *Complete Writings*. 2 vols. New York: Wise, 1929.

Engle, Edwin A. *The Haunted Heroes of Eugene O'Neill*. Cambridge: Harvard University Press, 1953.

Epstein, Arthur D. "A Look at *A View from the Bridge.*" In *Critical Essays on Arthur Miller,* edited by James J. Martine, 107–18. Boston: G. K. Hall, 1979. (First published in *Texas Studies in Literature and Language* 7, no. 1 [1965]: 109–22.)

Falk, Doris. *Eugene O'Neill and the Tragic Tension*. New Brunswick, N.J.: Rutgers University Press, 1958.

Falk, Signi. *Tennessee Williams*. Boston: Twayne, 1978.

Feidelson, Charles, Jr. *Symbolism and American Literature*. Chicago: University of Chicago Press, 1953.

Fergusson, Francis. "Melodramatist." In *O'Neill and His Plays: Four Decades of Criticism,* edited by Oscar Cargill et al., 271–82. New York: New York University Press, 1961. (First published as "Eugene O'Neill," *Hound and Horn,* January 1930.)

————. "Three Allegorists: Brecht, Wilder, and Eliot." *Sewanee Review* 64 (Autumn 1956): 544–73.

Ferres, John H. "Introduction." In *Twentieth Century Interpretations of "The Crucible,"* edited by John H. Ferres, 1–19. Englewood Cliffs, N.J.: Prentice-Hall, 1972.

Firebaugh, Joseph J. "The Humanism of Thornton Wilder." *Pacific Spectator* 4 (1950): 426–38.

Floyd, Virginia. *The Plays of Eugene O'Neill: A New Assessment*. New York: Ungar, 1985.

Frenz, Horst, ed. *American Playwrights on Drama*. New York: Hill and Wang, 1965.

Fuller, Edmund. "Thornton Wilder: The Notation of a Heart." *American Scholar* 28 (1959): 210–17.

Furness, R. S. *Expressionism.* London: Methuen, 1973.

Gassner, John. *Directions in Modern Theatre and Drama.* New York: Holt, Rinehart, Winston, 1965.

———. *Dramatic Soundings.* Edited by Glenn Loney. New York: Crown Publishers, 1968.

———. *Form and Idea in Modern Theatre.* New York: Dryden, 1956.

———. *Theatre at the Crossroads: Plays and Playwrights of the Mid-Century American Stage.* New York: Holt, Rinehart, and Winston, 1960.

———. *The Theatre in Our Times.* New York: Crown, 1954.

———, ed. *O'Neill: A Collection of Critical Essays.* Englewood Cliffs, N.J.: Prentice-Hall, 1964.

Gelb, Arthur, and Barbara Gelb. *O'Neill.* New York: Harper and Row, 1962.

Goldstein, Malcolm. *The Art of Thornton Wilder.* Lincoln: University of Nebraska Press, 1965.

Goldstone, Richard H. Interview with Thornton Wilder. In *Writers at Work: The Paris Review Interviews,* edited by Malcolm Cowley, 99–118. New York: Viking, 1958.

Granger, Bruce Ingham. "Illusion and Reality in Eugene O'Neill." *Modern Language Notes* 73, no. 3 (1958): 179–86.

Granville-Barker, Harley. *On Dramatic Method.* London: Sidgwick and Jackson, 1931.

Groff, Edward. "Point of View in Modern Drama." *Modern Drama* 2 (1959): 268–82.

Haberman, Donald. *The Plays of Thornton Wilder.* Middletown, Conn.: Wesleyan University Press, 1967.

Hartigan, Karelisa V., ed. *The Many Forms of Drama.* Lanham, Md.: University Press of America, 1985.

Hayman, Ronald. *Arthur Miller.* World Dramatists Series. New York: Ungar, 1972.

Highsmith, James Milton. "The Cornell Letters: Eugene O'Neill on his Craftsmanship to George Jean Nathan." *Modern Drama* 15 (1972): 68–88.

Hill, Phillip G. "*The Crucible:* A Structural View." *Modern Drama* 10 (1967): 312–17.

Jackson, Esther Merle. *The Broken World of Tennessee Williams.* Madison: University of Wisconsin Press, 1965.

———. "The Problem of Form in the Drama of Tennessee Williams." *CLA Journal* 4 (1960): 8–12.

Kaucher, Dorothy Juanita. "Modern Dramatic Structure." *University of Missouri Studies* 3, no. 4 (October 1928).

Kazan, Elia. "Notebook for *A Streetcar Named Desire.*" In *Twentieth-Century Interpretations of "A Streetcar Named Desire,"* edited by Jordan Y. Miller, 21–27. Englewood Cliffs, N.J.: Prentice-Hall, 1971.

Kermode, Frank. "Secrets and Narrative Sequence." *Critical Inquiry* 7 (Autumn 1980): 83–101.

———. *The Sense of an Ending.* London: Oxford University Press, 1966.

Kernan, Alvin B. "Truth and Dramatic Mode in the Modern Theater: Chekhov, Pirandello, and Williams." *Modern Drama* 1 (1958): 101–14.

Kerr, Walter. *Thirty Plays Hath November.* New York: Simon and Schuster, 1969.

Kolve, V. A. *The Play Called Corpus Christi.* Stanford, Calif.: Stanford University Press, 1966.

Kronick, Joseph G. *American Poetics of History.* Baton Rouge: Louisiana State University Press, 1984.

Krutch, Joseph Wood. *The American Drama Since 1918: An Informal History.* New York: Braziller, 1957.

———. *"Modernism" in Modern Drama.* Ithaca: Cornell University Press, 1953.

Kuhn, Thomas S. *The Structure of Scientific Revolutions.* 2d ed. Chicago: University of Chicago Press, 1970.

Lawson, John Howard. "Eugene O'Neill." In *O'Neill: A Collection of Critical Essays,* edited by John Gassner, 42–51. Englewood Cliffs, N.J.: Prentice-Hall, 1964.

———. *Theory and Technique of Playwriting and Screenwriting.* 1936. Reprint. New York: Putnam, 1949.

Lecky, Eleazer. "*Ghosts* and *Mourning Becomes Electra:* Two Versions of Fate." *Arizona Quarterly* 13 (1957): 320–38.

Lee, Robert C. "Eugene O'Neill's Remembrance: The Past is the Present." *Arizona Quarterly* 23 (1967): 293–305.

Lewis, Allan. "Arthur Miller—Return to the Self." In *American Plays and Playwrights of the Contemporary Theatre.* Rev. ed. New York: Crown Publishers, 1970.

Lewis, R. W. B. *The American Adam.* Chicago: University of Chicago Press, 1955.

Londre, Felicia Hardison. *Tennessee Williams.* World Dramatists Series. New York: Ungar, 1979.

Mabley, Edward. *Dramatic Construction: An Outline of Basic Principles.* Philadelphia, Pa.: Chilton, 1972.

Mander, John. *The Writer and Commitment.* London: Secker and Warburg, 1961.

Martine, James J., ed. *Critical Essays on Arthur Miller.* Boston: G. K. Hall, 1979.

———, ed. *Critical Essays on Eugene O'Neill.* Boston: G. K. Hall, 1984.

Miller, Arthur. *The American Clock.* London: Methuen, 1983.

———. *The Archbishop's Ceiling.* New York: Dramatists Play Service, 1985.

———. *Collected Plays.* 2 vols. 1957. Reprint. New York: Viking Press, 1981.

———. *Danger: Memory!* New York: Grove Press, 1986.

———. *The Theater Essays of Arthur Miller.* Edited by Robert A. Martin. New York: Viking Press, 1978.

Miller, Jordan Y., ed. *Twentieth Century Interpretations of "A Streetcar Named Desire."* Englewood Cliffs, N.J.: Prentice-Hall, 1971.

Miller, Perry. Introduction to "Benjamin Franklin and Jonathan Edwards." In *Major Writers of America,* edited by Perry Miller. New York: Harcourt, 1962.

Mishoe, Billy. "Time as Antagonist in the Dramas of Tennessee Williams." Ph.D. diss., Florida State University, 1972.

Murphy, Brenda. "Miller, Kazan, and Mielziner: American Drama as a Collaborative Art." Paper presented at the Modern Language Association annual convention, New York, 29 December 1986.

———. "O'Neill's Realism: A Structural Approach." *Eugene O'Neill Newsletter* 7, no. 2 (Summer/Fall 1983): 3–6.

Murray, Edward. *Arthur Miller, Dramatist.* New York: Ungar, 1967.

Nelson, Benjamin. *Tennessee Williams: The Man and His Work*. New York: Ivan Obolensky, 1961.

Nolan, Paul T. "Two Memory Plays: *The Glass Menagerie* and *After the Fall*." *McNeese Review* 17 (1966): 27–38.

Olivier, Sir Laurence. Letter to Arthur Miller. In *The Crucible: Text and Criticism*, edited by Gerald Weales, 153. New York: Viking, 1971. (First published in *Michigan Quarterly Review* 6 [Summer 1967]: 182.)

O'Neill, Eugene. *Long Day's Journey into Night*. New Haven: Yale University Press, 1956.

———. "Memoranda on Masks." *American Spectator*, November 1932, 3.

———. "O'Neill's Own Story of *Electra* in the Making." In *American Playwrights on Drama*, edited by Horst Frenz, 11. New York: Hill and Wang, 1965. (First published in *New York Herald-Tribune*, 3 November 1931.)

———. *The Plays of Eugene O'Neill*. 3 vols. New York: Random House, 1955.

———. *Ten "Lost" Plays*. New York: Random House, 1964.

———. *A Touch of the Poet*. New Haven: Yale University Press, 1957.

Opper, Hylbert Norman. "Exposition in the Plays of Eugene O'Neill." M.A. thesis, Northwestern University, 1937.

Överland, Orm. "The Action and Its Significance: Arthur Miller's Struggle with Dramatic Form." *Modern Drama* 18 (1975): 1–14.

Papajewski, Helmut. *Thornton Wilder*. Translated by John Conway. New York: Ungar, 1968.

Parker, Brian. "Point of View in Arthur Miller's *Death of a Salesman*." *University of Toronto Quarterly* 35 (October 1965): 144–57.

Parker, R. B. "The Circle Closed: A Psychological Reading of *The Glass Menagerie* and *The Two Character Play*." *Modern Drama* 28 (1985): 517–34.

Parmenter, Ross. "Novelist into Playwright: An Interview with Thornton Wilder." *Saturday Review of Literature* 18 (11 June 1938).

Poirier, Richard. *A World Elsewhere*. London: Oxford University Press, 1966.

Popkin, Henry. "The Plays of Tennessee Williams." *Tulane Drama Review* 4, no. 3 (March 1960): 45–64.

Popper, Hermine I. "The Universe of Thornton Wilder." *Harper's*, June 1965, 72–81.

Porter, Thomas E. *Myth and Modern American Drama*. Detroit: Wayne State University Press, 1969.

Quigley, Austin E. *The Modern Stage and Other Worlds*. London: Methuen, 1985.

Quinn, Arthur Hobson. *A History of the American Drama from the Civil War to the Present Day*. 2 vols. New York: Harper, 1927.

Raleigh, John Henry. "Eugene O'Neill." In *Sixteen Modern American Authors: A Survey of Research and Criticism*, edited by Jackson R. Bryer. Durham, N.C.: Duke University Press, 1974.

———. "Eugene O'Neill and the Escape from the Chateau d'If." In *O'Neill: A Collection of Critical Essays*, edited by John Gassner, 17–22. Englewood Cliffs, N.J.: Prentice-Hall, 1964.

———. *The Plays of Eugene O'Neill*. Carbondale: Southern Illinois University Press, 1965.

————, ed. *Twentieth Century Interpretations of "The Iceman Cometh."* Englewood Cliffs, N.J.: Prentice-Hall, 1968.

Rama Murthy, V. *American Expressionistic Drama.* Delhi: Doaba House, 1970.

Reising, Russell J. *The Unusable Past: Theory and the Study of American Literature.* New York: Methuen, 1986.

Ricoeur, Paul. "Narrative Time." *Critical Inquiry* 7 (Autumn 1980): 165–86.

Rogoff, Gordon. "The Restless Intelligence of Tennessee Williams." *Tulane Drama Review* 10, no. 4 (Summer 1966): 78–92.

Sacksteder, William. "The Three Cats: A Study in Dramatic Structure." *Drama Survey* 5 (Winter 1966–67): 253–66.

Said, Edward W. *Beginnings: Intention and Method.* New York: Basic Books, 1975.

Scally, William A. "Modern Return to Medieval Drama." In *The Many Forms of Drama*, edited by Karelisa V. Hartigan, 107–114. Lanham, Md.: University Press of America, 1985.

Scanlan, Tom. *Family, Drama, and American Dreams.* Contributions in American Studies, no. 35. Westport, Conn.: Greenwood Press, 1978.

Schvey, Henry. "Why American Plays Are Literature." Paper presented at the Modern Language Association annual convention, New York, 29 December 1986.

Schwerdt, Lisa M. "Blueprint for the Future: *The Emperor Jones.*" In *Critical Essays on Eugene O'Neill*, edited by James J. Martine, 72–75. Boston: G. K. Hall, 1979.

Scott, Winfield Townley. "*Our Town* and the Golden Veil." *Virginia Quarterly Review* 29, no. 1 (1953): 103–17.

Selmon, Michael. "Past, Present, and Future Converged: The Place of *More Stately Mansions* in the Eugene O'Neill Canon." *Modern Drama* 28 (1985): 553–62.

Shaw, George Bernard. *Shaw's Dramatic Criticism.* Edited by John F. Matthews. New York: Hill and Wang, 1959.

Sievers, W. David. *Freud on Broadway: A History of Psychoanalysis and the American Drama.* New York: Heritage House, 1955.

Smith, Harrison. "The Skin of Whose Teeth Part II." *Saturday Review of Literature* 25 (26 December 1942): 12.

Smith, John. *The Generall Historie of Virginia, New England, & the Summer Isles.* In *Travels and Works of Captain John Smith*, edited by Edward Arber and A. G. Bradley. Vols. 1–2. New York: Burt Franklin, 1910.

Sokel, Walter H. *The Writer in Extremis: Expressionism in Twentieth-Century German Literature.* Stanford, Calif.: Stanford University Press, 1959.

Stamm, Rudolf. "The Dramatic Experiments of Eugene O'Neill." *English Studies* 28 1947): 1–5.

————. "'Faithful Realism': Eugene O'Neill and the Problem of Style." *English Studies* 40 (1959): 242–50.

Stanton, Stephen S. "Introduction." In *Camille and Other Plays*, edited by Stephen S. Stanton, vii–xxxix. New York: Hill and Wang, 1957.

————, ed. *Tennessee Williams: A Collection of Critical Essays.* Englewood Cliffs, N.J.: Prentice-Hall, 1977.

Stephens, George D. "*Our Town*—Great American Tragedy?" *Modern Drama* 1 (1959): 258–64.

Straumann, Heinrich. "The Philosophical Background of the American Drama." *English Studies* 26 (1944–45): 65–78.

Stresau, Herman. *Thornton Wilder.* Translated by Frieda Schutze. New York: Ungar, 1971.

Szondi, Peter. *Theories des modernen Dramas.* Frankfurt: Suhrkamp Verlag, 1956.

Tharpe, Jac, ed. *Tennessee Williams: A Tribute.* Jackson, Miss.: University Press of Mississippi, 1977.

Tiusanen, Timo. *O'Neill's Scenic Images.* Princeton: Princeton University Press, 1968.

Tornqvist, Egil. *A Drama of Souls—Studies in O'Neill's Super-Naturalistic Technique.* New Haven: Yale University Press, 1969.

Trowbridge, Clinton W. "Arthur Miller: Between Pathos and Tragedy." *Modern Drama* 10 (1967): 221–32.

Twain, Mark. *Pudd'nhead Wilson.* New York: Harper, 1922.

Valgemae, Mardi. *Accelerated Grimace: Expressionism in the American Drama of the 1920s.* Carbondale: Southern Illinois University Press, 1972.

Van Laan, Thomas F. *The Idiom of Drama.* Ithaca: Cornell University Press, 1970.

Voelker, Paul. "Eugene O'Neill's Aesthetic of the Drama." *Modern Drama* 21 (1978): 87–99.

———. "What Is American About the American Drama?" Paper presented at the Modern Language Association annual convention, New York, 29 December 1986.

Waith, Eugene M. "Eugene O'Neill: An Exercise in Unmasking." *Educational Theatre Journal* 13 (1960): 182–91.

Watson, James G. "The Theatre in *The Iceman Cometh:* Some Modernist Implications." *Arizona Quarterly* 34 (1978): 230–38.

Weales, Gerald. "Arthur Miller." In *The American Theater Today,* edited by Alan S. Downer, 85–98. New York: Basic Books, 1967.

———, ed. *The Crucible: Text and Criticism.* New York: Viking, 1971.

———, ed. *Death of a Salesman: Text and Criticism.* New York: Penguin Books, 1977.

———. "Tennessee Williams' Achievement in the Sixties." In *Tennessee Williams: A Collection of Critical Essays,* edited by Stephen S. Stanton, 61–70. Englewood Cliffs, N.J.: Prentice-Hall, 1977.

Welland, Dennis. *Miller: A Study of His Plays.* London: Eyre Methuen, 1979.

Whitman, Robert F. "O'Neill's Search for a 'Language of the Theatre.'" In *O'Neill: A Collection of Critical Essays,* edited by John Gassner, 142–64. Englewood Cliffs, N.J.: Prentice-Hall, 1964. (First published in *Quarterly Journal of Speech* 16, no. 2 [1960]: 154–70.)

Wilder, Thornton. *The Alcestiad or A Life in the Sun.* New York: Harper and Row, 1977.

———. *American Characteristics and Other Essays.* Edited by Donald Gallup. New York: Harper and Row, 1979.

———. *The Angel That Troubled the Waters, and Other Plays.* New York: Coward-McCann, 1928.

———. *The Long Christmas Dinner and Other Plays in One Act.* New York: Coward-McCann; New Haven: Yale University Press, 1931.

———. "Some Thoughts on Playwriting." In *American Playwrights on Drama,* edited by Horst Frenz, 52–62. New York: Hill and Wang, 1965.

———. *Three Plays.* New York: Harper, 1957.

Williams, Raymond. *Drama from Ibsen to Brecht.* New York: Oxford University Press, 1969.

————. "The Realism of Arthur Miller." *Critical Quarterly* 1 (1959): 140–41.

Williams, Tennessee. *Dragon Country*. New York: New Directions, 1970.

————. *I Rise in Flame, Cried the Phoenix*. New York: New Directions, 1951.

————. *A Lovely Sunday for Creve Coeur*. New York: New Directions, 1980.

————. *Out Cry*. New York: New Directions, 1969.

————. *The Theatre of Tennessee Williams*. 5 vols. New York: New Directions, 1971–76.

————. *27 Wagons Full of Cotton, and Other One-Act Plays*. 1945. Reprint. New York: New Directions, 1953.

————. *Vieux Carré*. New York: New Directions, 1979.

Wilson, Edmund. "The Antrobuses and the Earwickers." *Nation* 156 (30 January 1943): 167–68.

Winther, S. K. "Strindberg and O'Neill: A Study of Influence." *Scandinavian Studies* 31 (1959): 103–20.

Winthrop, John. *The History of New England, 1630–1649*. Edited by James Savage. New York: Arno, 1972.

Wixon, Douglas Charles, Jr. "The Dramatic Techniques of Thornton Wilder and Bertolt Brecht: A Study in Comparison." *Modern Drama* 15 (1972): 112–24.

Young, Stark. "Eugene O'Neill's New Play." In *O'Neill: A Collection of Critical Essays*, edited by John Gassner, 82–88. Englewood Cliffs, N.J.: Prentice-Hall, 1964. (First published in *Immortal Shadows* [New York: Scribner, 1948], 61–66.)

Young, Thomas Daniel. *The Past in the Present: A Thematic Study of Modern Southern Fiction*. Baton Rouge: Louisiana State University Press, 1981.

Index

145

ADP-9206   2/9/99

PS
338
M44
S37
1989